Adam LoDolce

Being Alone SUCKS!

How to Build Self-Esteem,
Confidence, and Social Freedom to
Transform Your Dating and Social Life

Copyright © 2011 Adam LoDolce
Ultimate Social Freedom
All rights reserved.

ISBN: 1456491954
ISBN-13: 9781456491956

No part of this book may be reproduced in any form or by any electronic or mechanical means including information storage and retrieval systems, without permission in writing from the author. The only exception is by a reviewer, who may quote short excerpts in a published review.

The information presented herein represents the views of the author as of the date of publication. This book is presented for informational purposes only. Due to the rate at which conditions change, the author reserves the right to alter and update his opinions at any time. While every attempt has been made to verify the information in this book, the author does not assume any responsibility for errors, inaccuracies, or omissions.

While the cases presented herein are based on true events, many of the names and details have been changed for privacy.

Edited by Stephanie Mann

*This book is dedicated to my parents for their love and support,
and to my brother for his unwavering guidance.*

Contents

About This Book

Being alone sucks. It just does. The only thing that sucks more than being alone is *feeling helpless* about being alone. It's a feeling that's about as enjoyable as sucking on fish-oil-covered lollipops.

The good news is that when you picked up this book, you made a decision to make a change. You began the process of swapping out that unpleasant sensation for a completely new, invigorating feeling. When you finish this book, you'll know 99% more than anyone else in the world knows about dating and attraction. You know why? Because most people have far too much pride to admit to themselves that they need help. You, on the other hand, have already taken that first and hardest step toward success. Think of this as your first AA meeting - except you're super cool and (hopefully) not an alcoholic.

I wrote this book to help both men and women learn how to meet more people, and to teach them what to do once they've met them. You'll see that the three most critical steps to improving your dating life are increasing your self-esteem, finding confidence, and unleashing something known as your social freedom. Social freedom is the ability to say, feel, and act like your true self in any social situation without fear of rejection or failure. It's the key to overcoming social anxiety, which is typically the biggest barrier to approaching and talking to new people, and feeling completely comfortable with yourself when you do.

This book is a general guide for singles on how to improve their ability to find their match. It is not a do's-and-don'ts book – the purpose of it is for you to establish enough of a fundamental understanding of attraction and dating that you will know what to do in a wide variety of social situations without looking for outside guidance.

Plus, I assure you that there's never just *one* right answer to any question you might ask about what to do in dating, as it almost always depends on the circumstances. The smallest look, comment, or touch from a person can send drastically different signals about what the next move is depending on the situation (as you will learn, body language is a huge part of communication). Unfortunately there is just no mathematical science to dating. Instead it's more of a philosophy. This philosophy transcends your dating life and will apply to your entire outlook on who you are and how you interact with others. If you could build up your self-esteem, confidence and social freedom, how do you think your entire life would change? Once you see the change for yourself, you'll realize how far-reaching this philosophy really is.

This book will teach you that philosophy – it won't feed you hackneyed advice that will only work under ideal circumstances. For example, I will never tell you that you must call a person the day after you meet them; I will never tell you to always say certain phrases or to move your body in certain ways. Beware of this type of advice from anyone, especially from so-called dating experts, because this indicates that they have only experienced a few different types of scenarios and have passed judgments on what to do based on their limited experiences. I won't fill this book with inflexible advice like this because, once again, your approach to each social situation completely depends on your audience.

Although I won't be telling you specifics of what to do and what not to do, I will be giving you guidelines and exercises that you should try and live by throughout your dating life and beyond. This is not to say that you must follow every single piece of this book's content, but certainly put some thought into what the most critical improvement areas are for you.

Think about it this way: if you choose three concepts in this book to focus on for the next three months, and improve your dating skills by 50% for each technique, you will be 340% more attractive to a potential match. (Wait...didn't I say dating wasn't mathematical?) But seriously – if one small technique or tweak helps you land your next girlfriend or boyfriend, or even your future spouse, isn't it worth a try?

As I said before, this book is designed for both men and women. Gender roles in relationships and attraction are certainly different, but there are some fundamental themes and lessons that apply equally to both genders. In addition, having read a myriad of books on dating and attraction targeted at both men and women, I've actually found that I've learned a lot about how to improve myself by reading the books written for women. Guys, if you want to learn more about how women think, give *Cosmopolitan* a gander. Ladies, if you're trying to understand why men think the way they do, pick up a *Maxim* and I assure you that your eyes will open wide with newfound understanding. In short, read everything in this book as it will all be applicable for you regardless of your gender or sexual orientation.

Couch jockey warning:

Last – but certainly not least – I want to stress how important it is to actually use the advice you get from this book. I know that a portion of you will read this book, think about what you learned, maybe discuss it with a few friends, and then put it on the bookshelf as just another form of bygone entertainment. The concepts you'll learn about here are *not* just for entertainment; rather, they are meant to actually help you take charge of your life and make some real changes. Take the time. Practice the concepts. Take a risk. What do you really have to lose?

For those of you that have the courage to change, just remember that in anything you do the first step is always the hardest. When you decide that you want to start working out, I guarantee you that the first day in the gym will be the roughest. If it's not, then I assure you that you will at least be extremely sore the next day. If you're not, then a personal trainer would argue that you're not working out hard enough.

The same logic follows when working to improve your social life. As you begin to get over your dating phobias, you are going to need to push your mind as hard as you would push your body in the gym. Not only will you have to work hard, you'll also need to make sure that you are "working out" (dating) the *right* way to get the results you want.

Over time you'll actually begin to get addicted to meeting new people. You read that correctly: Pretty soon you'll be so comfortable with yourself that your addiction to socializing will grow as people will be magnetically attracted to you and your personality. Just stick with the program and you'll quickly discover what you are truly capable of.

Please visit www.UltimateSocialFreedom.com for more advanced products and programs to improve your dating success. Adam LoDolce is also available as a dating coach to help you with your specific needs.

My Journey

Understanding women did not come naturally to me. Quite honestly, I can't imagine that it actually comes naturally to anyone. When I was younger, I was certainly envious of those friends of mine that were considered "naturals" at dating. Having an "attractive" personality was something I always thought you either had or you didn't.

My social patterns began to form in elementary school, where I found myself rejected from the "cool" crowd. I wasn't wanted at the "super duper cool kids" table and I struggled to find a clique beyond my best friend, Rob. As I grew older and entered high school, my difficulties fitting in at school were compounded by a fear that I would never find the right girl to settle down with. You see, my mother works with divorced couples and, having heard all of the worst divorce stories you can imagine, I knew it was absolutely critical for me to find the right person. Even at such a young age I could see how important it was that I learn to conquer my social barriers, because I knew that I did not want to end up like the people in her stories.

Don't get me wrong, though, I thoroughly enjoyed high school. I met all of my closest friends during that time, most of whom I still socialize with today. I had my first encounters with girls, too – but I never got into any type of committed relationship. My confidence with girls was low because I never believed in my core that I deserved the highest quality girlfriend. I had a major confidence issue.

Once I graduated from high school I remember thinking to myself that college was the answer. It would be full of new people who didn't know the "Adam" that I was. I could completely reinvent myself. This was the "real Adam's" time to shine; it was time to build my own unique identity. (Everyone's seen the movies, right? Tons of people hooking up, having a great time, partying, and meeting the loves of their lives!)

College hit me like Bruce Lee. I wasn't one of the lucky few who immediately found their cliques, or their bright and shiny new identities. Because I struggled during my first year to make a good group of friends, I began to look inward, thinking that there was something wrong with me. In high school I had low confidence; in college I also had low self-esteem. I suddenly turned into being that guy who didn't get any girls in college. Alcohol became my "go to" self-medication used for breaking through the social barriers that held me back – which, as most of us know, is not a viable long- or short-term strategy for success in dating.

This is a picture of me in college.

So, since I didn't meet many girls in high school or college, everything was always focused instead on what I thought of as the *true* end goal: graduating, making a ton of money, buying a house, buying a cool car, and as a result having my perfect match come find me to make many, many beautiful babies. It was the perfect plan, right?

I wish this were as easy as it is in the movies, but it never is. It wasn't my fault though, right? I told myself that it was just my circumstances: "Everyone else is wrong; people just don't see me for who I really am." Thoughts like this would plague my mind as I began to analyze what the heck I was doing wrong. In hindsight, what I was doing wrong was not doing anything at all. I didn't have the guts to ever approach a woman and had no idea what to say if I ever did muster up the guts to approach her.

After college, I did end up getting into a relationship with a girl that I knew from high school. She was a very sweet and caring person and we remain friends to this day, but I always knew that I needed to focus on *me* first before I could focus on seriously dating or marrying a girl. My own insecurities about dating made it impossible to really settle down at that point in my life. I knew that I needed to work on myself before the rest of my life would fall into place.

Still, I didn't truly analyze the concept of attraction and dating until the day came when the relationship abruptly ended and I found myself thrown back to the wolves. It felt like college all over again, except ten times harder, because this time to meet people I had to be *proactive*. No longer could I meet girls by chance in my college classes. I worked in an all-male environment, was terrified to approach girls, and most of my girl "friends" no longer lived in the area. It was a very bleak time for me.

This is a picture of me after college.

Initially, I tried everything to get into a relationship again as quickly as possible, but I couldn't find anyone to get into a relationship with! I tried online dating and thought that I could create the online façade of a confident person. Unfortunately, once I got on the date the girl usually saw right through me.

This time in my life really sucked. I call it "The Dark Ages" and get the chills every time I think back on it. Being single just didn't feel natural at this age; I desperately wanted to have someone by my side when things went wrong and to celebrate the good things when times were great. What made it worse was that many of my friends were in relationships, making it hard to find other single "wingmen" to go out with.

And then came "The Enlightenment Period". It was one of those light-bulb moments. I decided to Google "dating advice" and stumbled upon a number of people who were dating gurus and experts. Who would've ever thought that such a profession existed? As it turned out, they were professing that someone could actually *learn* to get better at dating and attraction. They espoused that attraction was oftentimes a learned skill, and not necessarily a natural trait.

I figured, "Why not?" I'm a really easy sell so it didn't take much to hook me in.

And I really was hooked. I knew that this was my moment to do something big. I made a goal for myself that I would not just "try" this out; I would wholeheartedly commit to transforming my social life.

I spent two years approaching *thousands* of women of all sorts whenever I saw an opportunity. Short, tall, funny, boring, annoying, and passionate. They were producers, actresses, models, professors, students, teachers, and nurses. By the end, I had had at least a twenty-minute conversation with every type

11

of woman you could ever imagine. I've always loved extreme sports, and I soon found that approaching and conversing with complete strangers gave me a bigger adrenaline rush than any snowboard jump I've ever hit.

The most fascinating revelation was that practice made perfect! I was actually *learning* how to meet anyone at anytime and anywhere, and how to build attraction with them. I became hooked on the concept. I continued reading more and more and taking more programs and courses on the topic. It was engulfing my entire existence.

I went from being terrified to approach anyone, to chatting up everyone everywhere I went. I truly burst out of my shell. It was liberating! My outlook on my entire life was turned on its head. People thought I was nuts, I thought I was nuts, but the most fascinating part of the entire endeavor was how easy it was to meet someone once I had gotten past the initial fear of approaching them.

All areas in my life improved. My sales began to go through the roof and I was making more money in a month than most people make in a year because I really began to understand the dynamics of social interactions. I had total control of all of my relationships, I was no longer needy and seeking approval from people, and I was just genuinely happy.

But let's back up for a minute. How did all that happen, and so fast? At the time I really didn't understand what approaching women had to do with the sudden improvements in the other areas of my life. Eventually I realized – as you will, too – that once I had mastered building relationships (romantically, socially and professionally), so many worries that were seemingly unrelated to my love life began to disappear from my world. It truly made me realize that most (if not all) of our emotions in our lives stem from the state of our romantic relationships. Once you conquer this area in your life, petty problems become just that – petty. Then big problems become emotionally manageable. Your personal core becomes so solid that you begin to feel unbreakable and no one has power over you, except for yourself. It becomes liberating and intoxicating. You become strong enough to eliminate negative people from your life, and positive influences begin to fill the spaces they've left behind.

I came to a point where I was making well into six figures and still had the flexibility to go out and socialize almost every night. I really had it good. I had time to continue to focus on dating and attraction while making great money despite the greatest economic recession in decades.

But for some reason, this just didn't cut it for me. I knew now that I was equipped to take what I learned from this incredible experience and share it with the world. I was constantly advised to just enjoy my cushy job and relaxing life, but I knew I had to do something bold, something I would have *never* done in a million years had I not gone through this unbelievable journey of self-development.

And so I quit the dream job to become a professional speaker and dating coach. I wanted to pass on to you everything I've learned about meeting new people and dating. My newly acquired self-esteem, confidence and social freedom allowed me to make this move and to discover my real calling in life:

Helping others became my true passion.

I put in my notice for my executive job in Boston, and moved to Los Angeles to work with successful dating coaches to learn their style and their business. At the time I had no reputation, little public speaking experience and no idea what I was doing, but it was a new exhilaration. If I could capture the feeling I got when I would approach a stranger for the first time and multiply it times one hundred, then it would make up a small fraction of what I was feeling at this time. But I knew in my core that what I was doing was right and so I was able to manage my intense emotions.

In the end, I was right to make the bold move. I love my life and I'm pursuing my true passion instead of the fancy car and pocket of cash that I so mistakenly thought were keys to social success only a few years ago. So how does this relate to you? My story urges you to drop everything and take control of yourself and your own life. Sometimes it's easier to know what you need to *remove* from your life than it is to know what you need to pursue. I knew that I had to quit my job first, and then figure out my life second. If you want to be successful in dating, you must be passionate about yourself and your life, so step number one is to just:

Make things happen. Today.

Make it happen, whatever it is. Chances are you have one thing that you know that you should do today to drastically improve your life, but you're either paralyzed by fear or you lack the motivation to do it. Perhaps you need to take control of your dating life, and that's why you're reading this book. If that's the case, then congrats! Regardless, make your life happen *today,* or else you'll wake up with a spouse who hates you and a boss who demeans you at every conference call.

Take charge of your life or life will take charge of you.

Now onto how to make that happen. Follow me on the adventure of a lifetime.

Warmest Regards,

Adam LoDolce

Introduction

Have you ever taken a step back and wondered, "Why not me?"

Maybe you think to yourself, "How does the 'weird apple sauce girl/boy at the office find an incredible relationship, but I'm relegated to staying home on a Saturday night, watching *Seinfeld* re-runs?" You might wonder over and over again, "Why do I get all the bad luck?" Or you might be thinking, "All of my friends that are in relationships seem so confident that they've found *the one*. Why not me?"

It's not a good place to be in. Being alone *sucks!*

Alternatively, maybe you've had lots of success with meeting people and getting dates, but you're just not meeting the person who fits your personality and identity best. Dating is such a tricky process and it can be insanely difficult to figure out who is the right person for you at the right time.

The reality is that dating is hard, and finding a partner to spend the rest of your life with is an even more daunting task. It's easier to figure out where to invest a million dollars than it is to invest your entire life in a marriage – at least the money investment will usually only last a few years. Marriage is (ideally) for life and you're choosing the person you're going to spend more time with than anyone else on planet Earth. For many out there who can't even get a girlfriend or boyfriend, marriage is the least of their worries – it's all about finding happiness *today*. Perhaps even just getting out there, finding a date and being social is the road to happiness for you. From there, with the right tools, you'll be able to figure it out. It just depends on who you are and what your strengths are.

What's troubling is that many of us fall victim to staying in horrible relationships based on our insecure beliefs that sex and companionship will vanish into thin air if we are ever single again. There are millions of people in hugely unhealthy relationships right now that would break up with their partner in a heartbeat if they felt there were better options available to them.

I want you to imagine that you have the choice to be with anyone you ever desired.

I don't mean a specific person, but instead, a certain *quality* of person. How would this change your life right now? Look over to your side and imagine this type of person is there with you now and is madly in love with you.

Would your friends start looking at you differently? Would *you* start looking at *yourself* differently? The vast majority of us typically judge ourselves based on other peoples' interpretations of us, which can either be a confidence-booster or -breaker. Interestingly enough, obtaining a high degree of social freedom is actually intended to combat this belief. The moment you break through the barrier of caring what other people think about you, you will immediately have more opportunities to be with the type of person you desire most.

Here's the truth: Reading this book won't necessarily get you that one girl or guy you've been lusting after forever. If you told me that you were absolutely in love with Jenny or Brad and you only wanted help so that you could attract that one person, do you know what I would tell you? Go out and meet ten new people in the next month. Go on three or four dates and then see how you feel. Boost your confidence, tighten up your style, lose your focus on that one person, and then re-evaluate whether that person is right for you. I assure you that your infatuation with Jenny or Brad will dissipate faster than you think.

Having options is the single most important power one can develop over time. If you only have one specific dream to aspire to, or just one goal to reach, you'll almost always fail. If you keep telling yourself, "The only way I can be happy is if I live in Key West with $6 million in my bank account and a model for a spouse," then you will most likely live a life of abject misery.

Our brains always search for more reasons why we are *unhappy,* but rarely search for more ways to *be happy.* I can assure you that if by snapping your fingers you miraculously had that millionaire lifestyle, you would find a new reason to be unhappy. This same concept would apply to your situation if you actually *got* Jenny or Brad right now. You would almost certainly be disappointed once the initial infatuation faded away.

Are you living in a fantasy world?

So many guys and girls say, "Adam, you're taking all of the romance out of finding true love." I'm definitely not saying that you can't bump into someone and instantaneously fall in love, have children, and die together as a beautiful couple like in *The Notebook* (yes, I've seen it). But saying that I'm taking the romance out of finding love is like saying I'm taking all the luck out of getting wealthy. Sure, there are some people that stumble upon a great product or a great job that leads them to enormous wealth very quickly, but the majority of people work very hard and strategically to find the job that fits them the best. If Oprah Winfrey or Bill Clinton worked at your company when they were twenty years old, how long do you think it would take for them to get to the top? Not too long, because they would find every way possible to make their goal a reality.

So make your dating goals a reality. The key difference between finding wealth and finding love is that it is not considered socially normal for people to work strategically at dating, while our society encourages working strategically to land a job or star a new business. If you want to leave it to chance that you might meet your perfect match, then please do so by all means. But just realize that you really are taking a *chance*. You have the opportunity to increase the likelihood of finding your perfect match fifty-fold by controlling your own dating destiny rather than letting it control you. Would you rather be a lottery player – or the next Bill Gates?

The Fundamentals of Dating

Learning about attraction

Congratulations! You are one of the fortunate few who are willing to admit to themselves that they need help with their dating lives. It absolutely floors me that young people spend hundreds of thousands of dollars to go to college to learn how to succeed in their careers, yet schools don't even spend a second teaching students the fundamentals of how to meet new people and build healthy social lives. Isn't it amazing how so many of our problems and heartaches are caused by either a lack of options to choose from or our inability to leave unhealthy relationships out of fear of the dreaded "single" status on Facebook?

You need to realize immediately that learning how to become attractive is no different than losing weight or learning to play the guitar. The media bombards us with images of people who have flawless bodies and we're constantly shown the talent of masterful musicians and athletes. We think to ourselves, "Wow, they are so lucky they were born that way. They had the right genetics and the talent to succeed. I could never be that person." This sentiment is so common in our society that we are constantly being sold low-quality "self-help" programs claiming to have the "quick fix" for all our imagined problems. Just like in music and fitness, becoming more attractive takes work and persistence – along with the unbreakable belief that you can achieve greatness in your love life.

What's the hardest part about all of this?

When you're learning attraction techniques, expect that you'll get worse before you can get better. The reason you'll take a dip in results at first is that when you are trying new techniques, it will feel a little unnatural and counterintuitive. The newness of your uncharacteristic actions will make you come off to others as less confident than if you were just doing what feels most natural to you. Basically, in order to get the real you to come out of its hiding place, you'll need to improve and change the identity you're projecting to the world today, and that's no easy task – but it's possible.

Think about it this way: When a musician becomes a rock star overnight, those first few weeks will undoubtedly feel unnatural because they are in the process of transforming themselves into a radically new persona. Yet as time moves on that person will grow into their new identity and fall comfortably into their dream role of playing music for millions of people. In the end, they will be in a much better place than they were when they started.

Just remember that you can't make a judgment on whether or not something is working until you've tried it with many different people. Most people try things once, get rejected, and then immediately say, "Well, that didn't work. Let's go back to comfortable me!"

To avoid this counterproductive reaction, a major point to remember throughout this new learning process is:

> *Don't drop any strategy or technique until you've tried it at least five times.*

If the rock star gets booed off stage the first time they perform, should they change their tune? No. Maybe they didn't practice enough, or it's possible that they were performing for the wrong audience altogether!

So, what is attraction?

Attraction is an *emotion*. It's an emotion and a bodily reaction that's similar to adrenaline. You can't force yourself to feel it, nor can you avoid feeling it. There's no real logic involved in attraction and oftentimes logic and attraction are actually dueling forces. When you are deciding whom to commit to, you will usually deal with the logic versus attraction debate.

Here are some examples of being logical without attraction:

How many times have you heard your friends say, "He's incredible: smart, funny, charming, good looking. But I just don't have those types of feelings for him"?

Or do you ever find yourself saying, "My parents love her and she's so much fun but I'm just not into her"?

Within three to six months, people who pursue logical relationships without attraction will feel so frustrated they want to *explode*. It's just not a successful long-term strategy. Regardless of how much sense the relationship may seem to make, if you don't feel the emotion of attraction for someone then the relationship won't survive.

Here are some examples of illogical attraction:

"There's just something about him – I just can't get myself away from him. But he's so bad for me and he has a girlfriend already."

"She's so cute and fun. I can't stop thinking about her. But she lives on the North Slope of Alaska."

Attraction is such a powerful emotion that it can suck you into some completely irrational situations. If you're deeply attracted to someone but the relationship just doesn't make sense whatsoever, you will certainly want to seek advice from trusted friends and family before making any decisions. Remember, attraction is one of the deepest emotions you can feel and so it sometimes overrides every sensible cell in your brain.

> ***When seeking a relationship, try to find the right balance between logic and attraction.***

Here's the definition of attraction:

Attraction (ə-tră̆k'shə̆n) n.: The action of drawing forth a powerful, intimate and romantic emotional response from another person.

People can't decide to whom they're attracted. It happens all the time – you meet someone, you're attracted to them and the relationship is very logical, but he or she tells you that you two are better off "just being friends." The other person knows that you are the "right" person for them, but cannot choose to feel attraction for you. This is why the dreaded "friend zone" exists.

What's most fascinating about attraction – and the reason why my line of work currently exists – is that people cannot always choose whom they are *not* attracted to. Sure, they can try and reason with themselves and say, "That person isn't successful enough for me," or "That person isn't good looking enough," but the emotion of attraction will usually win over their hearts.

This is why you can succeed in dating and attraction just by understanding how to create this intense emotion. It's just like learning how to make people laugh: by practicing certain proven techniques, even the dullest person can make people laugh. Just as everyone has the capacity for **humor** inside of them, we all have **attractive identities** inside of us. When put together, these two qualities make up an **attractive personality**.

How do you build an attractive personality?

To improve your dating and social life and create a powerful attractive personality, you need to improve these three critical components:

1. **Self-Esteem:** This is your overall perception or evaluation of your own self-worth. It is your own opinion of who you are.

2. **Confidence:** Having the knowledge and practice to know that your course of action is the best or most effective for any given situation.

3. **Social Freedom:** This is the degree to which you are able to say, feel, or act like your true self in any social situation without fear of rejection or failure. This is being socially open and outgoing.

Every concept in this book relates to building your self-esteem, increasing your confidence, or expanding your social freedom. The perfect combination of all three of these traits will create an incredibly attractive personality and a successful dating life:

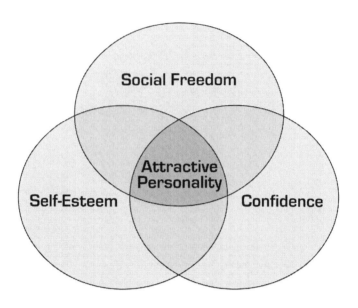

We all have varying degrees of each, but it is important to have *all three* working in combination with one another to build an attractive personality. Here are some examples of the consequences of lacking any part of this equation:

- If you ONLY have *social freedom*, then you will typically be considered awkward (no confidence) and will always be trying to prove something to everyone (no self-esteem).
- If you ONLY have *self-esteem*, then you will typically be very shy (no social freedom) and will only be able to connect with people after knowing them for a long time (no confidence).
- If you ONLY have *confidence*, then you won't be able to project your confidence to anyone (no social freedom) and you won't have any depth to your interactions (no self-esteem).

In a nutshell, you can build each of these aspects of attraction, and as you build one trait, you are certainly building on the others. Unfortunately, if you only focus on one trait and disregard the other two traits then you won't achieve excellence in any of them. Here's a breakdown of what I'll be covering in this book:

- **How to build self-esteem:** Setting personal goals and creating an attractive personal identity.
- **How to build confidence:** Learning what to say and how to say it.
- **How to build social freedom:** Consistently exposing yourself to social situations that are outside of your comfort zone.

It's also important to make sure that you:

Don't fall victim to Excusitis

It's completely natural for people to come up with a wide array of excuses to get out of trying something new, especially if there's risk of feeling pain during the learning process. Don't fall victim to the plague of "Excusitis." This is the disease of always having excuses about why you shouldn't change or improve yourself. If you want to do something in your life, *now* is always the time to do it. If you're reading this book, you want to take a stand and take control of your dating life. The only thing that will stop you is your list of excuses.

So, to help you avoid Excusitis, what I've done is compiled a list of the Top Five Excuses people come up with for not learning attraction or dating techniques and then the truth behind them:

1. **"It's just not me." Truth:** Many of our beliefs about dating are products of marketing, television, and how we were raised. Once you get rid of your chains, you will be free to be your true self. And then there's no going back.

2. **"I'm not good-looking enough." Truth:** Having worked in the dating and attraction field for some time now, I have seen some of the least attractive people date and marry the most beautiful, intelligent and high-value people you could imagine. Musicians, artists, professors, models – you name it – will all overlook your physical setbacks if you provide them with the most powerful emotions they've ever felt.

3. **"I keep getting rejected. How could this possibly be good for my self-esteem?" Truth:** It's counter-intuitive, but the more you get rejected, the more you will build your self-esteem. Maybe not at first, but over time you will grow immune to rejection and realize that it has nothing to do with the inner you.

4. **"Approaching strangers is 'creepy.'" Truth:** No, it's not. Maybe at first you might make people feel uncomfortable because *you* are uncomfortable, but once you break through this barrier I assure you that very few people will be unhappy to meet you. What's really the difference between getting introduced to someone and just introducing yourself?

5. **"This is manipulative." Truth:** I firmly believe that you're more likely to be manipulative *if you don't* build your attraction skills and just go on as you are today. People are manipulative when they feel that they can't get something by being honest and forthright.

If you have other excuses about making a change in your life that constantly plague your mind, write them down and try playing devil's advocate: Just think of *any* reason why your excuse is wrong. When it comes to making a major change, you are generally your own worst enemy. What's the harm in trying something new? Clearly, you are not happy with the way things are now. The worst thing that can happen is that you'll end up no better off then you currently are – however, I guarantee you even that won't happen.

Just have fun

Expanding your ability to date can be a terrifying experience or it can be exhilarating. Usually it's both. Learning to enjoy this process of discovering yourself and other people is critical to your success. The most fundamental thing to keep in mind is to:

JUST HAVE FUN!

Don't take this game too seriously and learn to laugh when things don't go the way you expect. As you build your own self-esteem you'll become far less dependent on the outcomes of social situations. You won't let other people dictate your own self-worth and you'll be able to find the humor in almost any situation.

Plain and simple, a key reason for us to be here on Earth is to seek happiness and have fun. This doesn't mean that volunteering at a local shelter or saving the environment isn't important, but if it doesn't make you happy, then I assure you that you won't stick with it. Sure, it may not seem fun waking up at

7:00 AM to feed the homeless breakfast, but the *feeling* you get from completing such activities is what justifies it. If you don't get *pleasure* from the things you do, I assure you that you won't do them consistently.

The same thing applies to improving your dating skills. I've met hundreds of men and women who just say, "I hate the dating scene; it's so annoying and hard. Why can't it just be over?" The reason why people have this reaction to dating is because they automatically associate far more pain with the act of meeting new people and being single than the pleasure of the excitement and anticipation of potentially meeting a mind-blowing person who will forever change you. Everything we do in life is either pursuing pleasure or avoiding pain, so discover the pleasure in dating and you will inevitably become more successful at it.

Maybe it's sex. Maybe it's companionship. Maybe it's kissing. Maybe it's laughing. Maybe it's crying! Whatever it is, just find something about dating that is fun for you and focus on it. Find a way to make the positives outweigh the negatives in learning how to date and socialize.

The fun part of all of this is that every time you walk out the door you have an opportunity to discover something or someone you never knew existed. I have traveled around the world numerous times in search of unique and exciting experiences, but until I really began to get enormous pleasure out of meeting people, I didn't realize that each person I meet is a *world* unto himself. You really don't have to travel far to discover a new galaxy of experience. You can go to the local grocery store and discover three new planets fresh perspective that you never knew existed until that moment. Every person you walk by on the streets has a unique story and something to teach you about yourself.

*Having fun with this learning process is
critical to your success.*

Have you ever noticed those days when you just wake up on the wrong side of the bed and nothing is fun to you? And then everyone comes up to you and asks you, "What's wrong? You look so upset!" The reality is that we cannot hide our true emotions completely. Sure, you can use many of the body language techniques that are outlined further in this book, but unless you actually begin enjoying the act of meeting people then the highest quality prospective mates will still see right through you.

Most people perceive the concept of "fun dating" as a Catch-22. They say, "What can I do? I can't have fun unless people like me, and you're telling me that I can't get people to like me unless I have fun." The simple truth is that when you're dating and meeting new people, *you can't focus solely on the results*. Focus on what makes you laugh and have fun while you're trying out new things that may make you feel uncomfortable.

For example, I had a dating coaching client that finds it fun going to Red Sox games at Fenway Park, but generally hates approaching women. I told him to focus on what's fun: baseball games. Then, as a side note, to keep a peripheral view of prospective women and just start conversations with people about fun topics. He then started meeting a few women at the park and he gained more confidence and social freedom, which ultimately caused him to have a lot more fun with it. So now when he goes to non-sporting events to meet women, he still has the "fun" association of meeting people based on his experience at Fenway.

Most importantly, *everyone else just wants to have fun*. If there's one thing you take away from this book it's that people just want to laugh and be comfortable when you're with them. I've been on dozens of dates when the girl wants to take the date very seriously and this is not only unattractive to me, but inevitably I will be unattractive to her if I reciprocate. The first thing I'll do in this situation is change the mood and focus on *me* having fun, and ultimately she joins and has a night full of laughs and silly jokes.

Focus on you first, and everyone else will join.

A positive personality is contagious! Be the person who lights up the room and you'll see everyone start to feel more comfortable around you. A person who exudes confidence and social freedom puts other people at ease because they don't feel like they're being judged. Instead, they feel as though you are there to have a good time and are open to all types of people.

The effects of alcohol

I'm not going to preach to you about the harmful and dangerous effects of alcohol because you probably know how bad alcohol abuse can be. Furthermore, I'm not vehemently against drinking in *moderation* when you're out socializing, as long as you are of age. However, it is absolutely worth mentioning that many people's biggest problem in building attraction and meeting the right people is that they drink too much at social gatherings. Too much alcohol makes you say the wrong things at the wrong times, reduces your ability to convey the right body language, and can cause you to make bad decisions. Engaging in binge drinking will virtually guarantee that you won't meet someone who is of the quality you deserve.

Alcohol is almost everyone's first choice of a social lubricant. It gets you to say gutsier things than you normally would, and gives you the false confidence to do things you would never do if you were sober. Unfortunately, drinking alcohol doesn't build sustainable self-esteem, confidence or social freedom. Perhaps you might have a night out where you look confident and are socially free, but where does that leave you in the morning? Usually on the couch eating Doritos and chugging water.

My suggestion for alcohol is to use it in moderation or even not at all as you begin learning more about improving yourself socially. Once you have transformed yourself into a dating master, feel free to drink however you'd like, but for now, I recommend keeping it to a minimum.

Now let's start with the most fundamental part of building ourselves to become more attractive to others.

Building Self-Esteem: Shaping Your Unique Concise Identity

Before we work on the specific techniques you will use to build attraction, we need to review the **identity** that you put forward when you're meeting people. Without a solid identity (what it is that makes you unique; essentially your "personal brand") you will not be able to retain high-quality people while dating or while in relationships. This section is designed for you to build a more concise and defined personality.

Goals and ambitions

Our goals and ambitions are what give us purpose on this earth. The greatest buildings, songs, paintings and movies are the results of people stretching their own abilities to create something bigger than themselves. For today's purposes, you don't want to build or paint anything, but you do want to find an exciting and fulfilling relationship – arguably a harder task than anything else. Ever hear of how Vincent van Gogh cut his ear off and sent it to his girlfriend? I'm sure at that moment he would've rather had a mastery of dating than a mastery of the paintbrush.

We are all just trying to find our small place on Earth and our own moment in time. As you're reading right now, I'm sure you can probably think of at least three goals you want to achieve (outside of money or possessions) that would make you even more attractive to others and make you feel more personally fulfilled. The key to success in the dating world is to first improve your unique identifiers and then learn how to *emphasize* them in every interaction. It is critical to define your Unique Concise Identity (UCI) because this is essentially a snapshot of what defines you as a person. In order to know others, you must first know yourself. Having a strong sense of identity leads to higher confidence, which in turn attracts more people.

Having a Unique Concise Identity leads to attracting high-quality people.

It's not possible to date and retain a high-quality partner without having a strong and attractive identity. Men: No supermodel or actress will continue to date you just because you seemed confident when she first met you. Women: No rock star or pro football player will continue to date you just because you're a great flirt. High-quality people want depth and you must continue to build yourself not only to improve your dating life but also to enhance your overall quality of life.

As your dating advisor, I'm not going to trick you into believing that you can just say and do all the right things in any given conversation to land the person of your dreams. You need to back it up with real content:

- I'm not saying that you need to be a multi-millionaire to keep a relationship, but you should have enough to support yourself and have a job that you are passionate about.
- I'm not saying that you need to be the next Slash, but if you love music then pick up the guitar immediately and cultivate your talents and hobbies.
- I'm not saying that you need to be Shaun White, but if you talk about your passion for extreme sports, plan a trip to go snowboarding.

Being passionate about something – anything – is almost as attractive as being successful at doing it. If you love to dance and are insanely passionate about it, but in reality are not a great dancer, you can still make "dancing" your core identity.

Now it's time to start pursuing your goals because:

In the blink of an eye, you will be married.
In another, you will be dead.

Death and marriage should be your two greatest motivators to make a change in your life today. By reading this book, I'm assuming that you want to get married someday and spend the rest of your life with one person. You have a very short time in life to do whatever it is that makes you happy – so do it now, don't hesitate, and just have fun with it. Once you have a family, it's going to be infinitely harder to make the time to focus on *you*.

An old proverb that my Grandpa LoDolce always said was:

Some people make things happen, some watch things
happen, while others wonder what has happened.

Don't wake up as an elderly person in a rocking chair and wonder what has happened. Do it for yourself, your future spouse, and your future children: *Make things happen, today*.

Exercise:
List three activities you've always wanted to do:

1: _____
2: _____
3: _____

What are your passions in life? Make a list of your hobbies/activities that you believe are attractive.

Passion 1: _____
Passion 2: _____
Passion 3: _____

Note: Find someone who's really good at your passion, model that person, and then find a way to get paid for doing something you love.

Following the rules

Simply put, you are a 100% custom-made person and there is no one in the world like you. No one has the same thoughts, the same clothing, the same hobbies, the same reactions, the same family, or the same background as you. So why should you have to do the same things everyone else is doing and follow their rules?

Those who follow the rules don't make the rules.

We've been raised to always follow the rules or else we get punished. Now that we are past the age of having official "rules" to follow, we can choose to either follow other people's rules or create our own. Living by your own rules and your own guidelines will inevitably cause others to follow suit. Your degree of social freedom will dictate your ability to create these rules. As you begin to expand your social freedom, you'll see that you'll become more of an individual. The more you define the rules through the power of your personality and your confidence, the more you will lead instead of follow others.

Ask yourself: Who is more attractive, a leader or a follower?

Building your Unique Concise Identity

Your Unique Concise Identity should be a reflection of who you are today, and who you want to be tomorrow. Furthermore, your UCI should be attractive to others. Having a well-crafted identity is such an effective way to build *quick* attraction because people can immediately associate you with a particular category, and all of the positive emotions they associate with that type of person can be directed towards you. Having a sexy UCI allows you to build immediate attraction within the first ten minutes of a conversation. When you have a powerful UCI, people can tell immediately whether they like you or not, and this process rapidly weeds out the people who aren't right for you.

For example, I once dyed my hair black and got a strange piercing on my left ear, and didn't even realize it, but I immediately looked very much like Adam Lambert (especially because I dress kind of like a rocker). For those of you who don't know Adam Lambert, let me save you time – he's a rocker and actor who became famous on *American Idol.* He also happens to be homosexual. Interestingly enough, because he is gay, he's highly desirable to women: He's good looking, high-value, and women can never have him!

So, within three minutes of a conversation, people couldn't help but say, "Hey, you kind of look like Adam Lambert." Now, most heterosexual guys would probably say, "Oh no! Do I?" and get self-conscious about their look. Instead, on queue I would do a Michael Jackson kick and spin around and say, "Well, I can't sing like him, but I did teach him how to dance."

Because it got a positive reaction every time, this was one of my silly conversational routines that stuck over time. For a girl who liked rock-and-roll guys I was the perfect catch because I had a UCI that was sexy to her. Alternatively, I would turn off girls who were not into edgier and more adventurous guys like me, which was fine because I really wasn't interested in them. Having a UCI helps you to quickly separate those who are not compatible with you with those that are. See how this works?

I've now changed my style a bit and no longer look so much like Adam Lambert, but I still do have a rocker identity. I love rock music, I play the guitar and I ride a motorcycle. These qualities were all a part of me before I even learned attraction, so it seemed like it was only natural to have my Unique Concise Identity include a rock and roll vibe. If you had spoken to me two years ago, you would've had no idea that I had these more "unique" interests. Now, within one minute of meeting me, someone is able to see all those aspects of my personality.

When I coach someone in dating, the very first thing I have my client do is work on his or her own UCI. For example, I recently worked with someone named John. We had a conversation, and I began with, "John, tell me about yourself."

He responded with, "Well, I listen to music, I like to go hiking, and – umm – I'm an engineer."

I said, "Ok, then let's tighten this up. What type of music do you listen to?"

John: "I listen to everything."

Adam: "Come on John, if there was *one* type of music you would listen to for the rest of your life, what would it be?"

John: "I suppose it would be rock and roll."

Adam: "Ever play an instrument?"

John: "Yes, guitar. But I'm really not that good."

Adam: "Ok, great. That doesn't matter for now! Now let's talk about hiking. Why do you enjoy hiking?"

John: "Well, I like the great outdoors and I like to walk around a lot."

Adam: "So do you enjoy the adventure of hiking? Do you like the exploration of new environments? Do you like to travel?"

John: "Yes, I enjoy all of that. Definitely. That's why I like hiking."

Adam: "Ok, then let's drop the engineer bit for now. Your new Unique Concise Identity is: John is a rocker who plays guitar and has a passion for adventure and traveling the world."

John: "But isn't that a bit of a stretch? I mean – I'm not really comfortable with that."

Adam: "Don't worry, you will be. Now, the first things you need to do are pick up guitar lessons and book a trip somewhere to travel. We need to fulfill this identity. It is what you want, right?"

John: "Yes, yes it is."

So what's more attractive?

1. **John's old identity:** An engineer who listens to music and hikes.
2. **John's new Unique Concise Identity:** A rocker who plays guitar and has a passion for adventure and traveling the world.

Most people would agree that number two is more attractive.

Make stereotypes work for you, not against you.

We all stereotype! So why not actually make it work for you? You can either be stereotyped as a Gap-wearing middle manager, or as a:

- Rock and roller
- DJ
- Artist
- Hipster
- Wall Street executive
- Chic male/female
- Prep
- Grunge rocker
- Nerd (yes, if done right, nerdy can be sexy!)
- Surfer/skateboarder/adrenaline junky
- Intellectual

Whatever you do, make sure you represent the stereotype more extremely than others do. At first it may feel uncomfortable representing a new UCI. It won't feel like the real you, because there's always contradiction in our identities, such as being a rock and roller but working as a software developer. You may feel a little fake at first, a little outside of your comfort zone, but stick with it. If you continue to work at it, your UCI will become *you*, and all other less interesting areas of your life will fall to the side when you are interacting with people.

Your Unique Concise Identity will be a part of how you talk, feel, and look as you continue to build yourself towards successful dating.

Don't get me wrong – if you are a software developer, for example, and that is your most interesting identity, then you should roll with it. If your UCI is not usually considered sexy by most standards, you can certainly still present it in an attractive manner. Fit the profile and go with the software hacker, chic nerd persona. Just accentuate who you are to the extreme. When you describe what you do, you could say something like, "There is something so incredible about developing code – I can't even describe it. Every line I create is getting me one step closer to a final product that I know will change how people live their lives. It will make them that much happier from day to day and that's why developing software has become my true *passion.*" Just conveying that you are proud and *passionate* about what you do will help you build attraction despite having a job as seemingly boring to the outside world as developing code.

I should add that although it's important to be congruent with your UCI when you initially meet people, as you begin dating someone you can certainly fall out of your stereotype and this can build even more attraction. For example, if a man has stereotyped a woman as being a grunge rocker, but then later finds out that she loves classical music and dances to ballet, this will inevitably be *more* attractive because it's unexpected and surprising. Or for example, if a guy is a motorcycle rider stereotype, but a woman later finds out that he volunteers at a retirement home, this will typically build intense attraction as many women would find this as endearing. It's all about mysteriousness: leave them wondering at all times who you are and make them excited to get to know more about the depth of your personality.

In a nutshell, the key to stereotyping is to ensure that early on in your interactions you have a very *congruent* and *concise* identity, and then after your initial interaction you can provide subtle hints to your alternative identities to build even more attraction. Being able to peel away the layers of your personality is invigorating for anyone. Just be sure not to peel it all away in the first interaction!

Exercise

Describe your identity today (how would describe yourself to other people?)

_____
_____
_____
_____

Describe who you *want* to be (Unique Concise Identity):

_____
_____
_____
_____

What is one thing you can do *today* to achieve your Unique Concise Identity? (Go do it!)

_____

List three goals you need to achieve in the next three months to feel confident in your new identity:

Goal 1:_____

Goal 2:_____

Goal 3:_____

Find a famous person who also fits this sexy identity. This is your identity role model:

Famous Person with my Unique Concise Identity: _____

Note: Read their story and their background. What did they do to get to their level of fame? Begin modeling their behavior.

Clothing and style

Your clothing should reflect your Unique Concise Identity. It is a critical part of becoming more attractive to others.

So why do most people dress within the social norm?

First, blame your parents.

Most of us learn fashion initially from our parents. Women get their style from their mothers who usually spend money on jewelry and fashion designer clothing. Men dress like nice guys because this is what they are told to do in order to emulate their fathers.

Basically, we're told that we should stay within the boundaries of what's socially acceptable.

If your parents think you look nice in your shirt,
it doesn't mean you look attractive in your shirt.

The safest way to go on in life is to just wear the clothing that everyone else is wearing. You will get noticed far less often and run almost no risk of rejection.

The second reason why we dress within the norm is due to the "elementary school syndrome."

We all knew that kid who was never up on the latest trends, or that girl that cut her hair way too short. I'll never forget in elementary school when a girl I knew, Jenny, cut her hair too short. Even though Jenny was very pretty and cool everyone still made fun of her for months! These kids would get tormented beyond belief; their lives were nothing but pure misery until they conformed to the rest of the kids. Jenny would certainly think twice before cutting her hair short again. I bet she hasn't done it since then.

Interestingly enough, as we grow older something strange happens. There becomes a premium on dressing outside of the norm, because all of the sudden it's considered unique and interesting. Those people who have the guts to confidently go out wearing something different are the ones who attract others the most.

So why is clothing so important when it comes to attraction?

When you meet someone for the first time, you make snap judgments about them based on the way they look and present themselves. You do this to answer the natural question, "Is this someone worth talking to?"

Important notice: You do not need to spend thousands of dollars to dress attractively!

One of the biggest mistakes that men and women make in fashion is thinking that the more they spend on clothing, the more attractive they will be. If you expand your social freedom and dress outside the norm, you will save a ton of money on clothing and be far more attractive than 95% of people out there. Fashion outlets like H&M allow you to buy interesting clothing for inexpensive prices.

Traditionally, women know how to dress fashionably, and men know how to dress like "nice guys." These types of styles do not usually create transformational success in dating as they fit in with the social norm. The most effective way to quickly attract high-quality prospective partners is to be congruent with your UCI.

*First impressions count, but fulfilling
your impression counts more.*

If you represent yourself as a chic nerd, then you better be telling stories about math or science. If you are dressed as a rocker, don't start your initial interaction with, "So when I was hanging with my grandma..." Make your very first impression a mile deep, then fill that mile with your personality, stories, and confidence that back up your Unique Concise Identity. As I mentioned previously, congruence with your UCI is important during your first interaction so that people can easily stereotype you.

Keep in mind that if you do happen to hang with your grandma regularly, people will actually find this appealing if you share this with them as they get to know you better. Absolute congruence with your UCI is only crucial during the initial "attraction" phase of the relationship.

As far as clothing is concerned:

*A sexy style is a concise snapshot of
your Unique Concise Identity.*

"Concise" is the key word here. You won't want to be everything to everyone. If you don't have a Unique Concise Identity, it will be obvious to others when they look at you.

Men don't usually take much notice when women dress in high-fashion clothing. They *do* notice when women accent their personality through their clothing.

Women notice when men dress in high fashion, but they're most attracted to men who are comfortable enough to dress outside of the social norm and show their identity.

One more thing to keep in mind:

Dress the part and you will become the part.

Altering your clothing style is the easiest way to improving your self-esteem and increasing your self-worth. If your clothing aligns with your UCI, your personality will naturally follow, as people will just expect you to act a certain way. If you want to be a rock star then dress like a rock star. If you want to be an athlete, then dress like an athlete. Make sure your personality and clothing are completely aligned to create a concise, attractive identity.

Put in so much effort to your clothing that it looks effortless.

It's generally not a positive thing to look like you spent four hours getting ready (especially if you're a guy). The key to your style is to put so much thought into what you're wearing that it looks like you just threw it on in ten minutes.

Last but certainly not least, it is important to exercise, eat right, and groom yourself accordingly. I'm not a health expert and don't expect you to go out and get abs like The Situation in *Jersey Shore*, but there is a certain level of attractive physical appearance that you must begin working to achieve. If you're overweight, then in order to build your self-esteem it's important to at least begin taking steps towards getting in shape. I recommend doing a Weight Watchers (www.weightwatchers.com) or Live Strong (www.Livestrong.com) program, through which you can monitor your exercise and calorie intake to achieve your goals.

As far as grooming is concerned, keep in mind the following:

- **Hair is very important because it's one of the first things people notice about you**: Once you find your sexy role model and the haircut you desire, bring a picture to your stylist, and have them snip accordingly.
- **Trim your facial/nose hair**: For men, I generally recommend less-to-no facial hair unless it's directly congruent with your identity (lumberjack?). If so, trim everything and keep it neat. For women – no facial hair, please.
- **Scent**: Your smell can be a very powerful pheromone, so be sure to wear the appropriate amount of cologne or perfume that complements your own body scent.
- **Breath and teeth:** Bad breath is usually a deal breaker when you're meeting people. Always bring gum or mouthwash everywhere you go. Also, it's generally a good idea to whiten your teeth every six months or so (whitening strips can be purchased at almost any supermarket or convenience store) to keep your teeth looking white and clean.

By getting in shape and cleaning yourself up, you will instantaneously be improving your own self-image and self-worth. This will inevitably improve your confidence and social freedom later on down the line. Take these things seriously because I assure you that the high-quality people whom you want to attract will!

Exercise:

Find five attractive pictures of the identity role model you chose in the previous section. Go shopping and purchase a few items of clothing that he/she is wearing.

Go out and wear them!

Identity on Facebook

Once you've gotten your identity down and feel more comfortable representing it in social surroundings, be sure to make your Facebook and social media sites align accordingly. Facebook can be a useful tool for building "comfort" with someone after you've met them and providing more evidence of your Unique Concise Identity.

There are a few fundamental suggestions to keep in mind if you are using Facebook to support your identity and build comfort with someone you've recently met:

- **Wall posts**: Make sure you have more wall posts than status updates. Show that you are popular by having lots of wall posts from your friends. The easiest way to do this is to post on other people's walls frequently so that they'll respond on yours.
- **Tagged photos**: Hide your tagged pictures and only show profile pictures. Tagged pictures are not always flattering, so in this case, less is more.
- **Relationship status:** I don't recommend using the relationship status. Generally having a relationship status of "single" portrays neediness.

Now that we've got the basics, the next step is to align your Facebook page to your UCI. This is where you can market yourself as a concise brand to be presented to the world. If you choose to be a DJ identity, but your musical preference shows all classical music, you are being incongruent with your personality and this is generally confusing. Even if you love classical music, choose the music to present to the world that goes along with your identity. Perhaps house music might be a better choice there? Remember, you shouldn't hide anything about yourself, but instead just emphasize those things that align with your UCI.

Your profile pictures should also stay within the basic frame of your identity. If you do not have many pictures of your new look, this is up to your discretion.

The benefit of using Facebook is that it can help you to create a closer connection with someone who might not be willing to meet with you in person yet, but is still interested in getting to know you. Basically, you can build enormous amounts of comfort with people if your Facebook page passes muster.

Identity on dating sites

I'm not a strong believer in using dating sites as your *primary* form of meeting people as they really don't build your self-esteem, confidence or social freedom. As you've already learned, without these traits it's very difficult to attract and retain high-quality partners. Furthermore, even if you get lots of dates through online sites, if you don't have these aspects of attraction covered, it will generally be difficult to get intimate or build a relationship with someone. With that said, you should certainly leverage online dating as a secondary tool for meeting new people as you develop these traits in organic social situations. I recommend using www.OKcupid. com because it's free and is really just as good as any other paid site I've seen.

Just like Facebook, your online dating profile should represent your new Unique Concise Identity. Remember, make it concise, and don't try to be everything to everyone.

Here are four basic tips to enhancing your online dating life:

1. **Get professional pictures:** Once you have a solid style that aligns with your identity, hire a professional photographer to take pictures of you in cool and interesting poses. Bring a few different pairs of clothes and try some artistic poses. Before you meet with the photographer, do some research and check out www.Flickr.com for ideas for pictures. Both men and women agree that the picture is the most important factor when someone is deciding whether they want to talk to you. Professional pictures will show you in the best light, the coolest poses, and will even make people wonder why you have professional photos (which will make you seem more interesting). On a lot of dating sites you can write a description of the picture, and if it's a professional picture, just write underneath "Professional photo shoot for work." Keep them wondering!

2. **Quantity is king:** Have patience and message everyone! The more you message people, the more success you will have. Be sure to mention something about the person's profile in your message and relate it to your identity.

3. **Always be the selector:** Make it abundantly clear the type of people you are *not* interested in. For example, write in your "likes" profile, "I'm adventurous and outgoing, so if you're boring and hate having fun, do NOT message me. We won't get along." This not only defines your identity but also lets people know that you have options.

4. **Don't be serious or needy:** Even if you're looking for the most passionate and committed relationship in the world, just remember one thing: People just want to have *fun!* It is not necessary to go into depth about the "seriousness of your need to be in a relationship" when you are writing your profile. This will turn off most of the desirable people in online dating (and real-life dating for that matter).

Once you have a meet-up confirmed, the rules of attraction differ ever so slightly with online dating. Because you've never met the person before, the very first thing that you want to do is build an enormous amount of *comfort* with each other. This can be done by simply finding commonalities and talking about your own passions. Once you have built comfort, then move on to building *attraction*.

Exercise

Visit www.Okcupid.com and set up an account. Spend a few hours going through dating profiles and try to find the most enticing profiles. Steal their material! If you see something funny or interesting you'd like to use, then why reinvent the wheel?

Building Self-Esteem:

Managing Your Mind

Now that we've worked on your Unique Concise Identity to improve your own self-image, it's time to learn how to regulate your own thoughts during and after social interactions.

It's important to realize that you are a unique and attractive person. This section is completely focused on targeting how your brain perceives yourself and those around you.

Be attracted to yourself to live a life full of love.

Regulating rejection

Our belief systems control our every thought, decision, action, and emotion.

Since you took your first breaths on Earth, your brain has been shaped by your DNA, your family environment, your society, and by your friends. You're constantly told what to do, what not to do, what's weird, and what's normal. These are typically the guidelines that drive us through our lives. We all have a tendency to make assumptions about everything, which is what helps us grow and learn. But nothing is ever as it seems.

It's not the individual events that happen in your life that shape who you are; rather, it's how you *interpret and react to* those events.

As you continue to expose yourself to others, you'll realize that there are only two possible outcomes when you have an "unsuccessful" interaction (such as a rejection):

1. **Learning experience:** If it is glaringly obvious what you are doing wrong, try to correct it. Be careful here, though: Many times we'll interpret an external factor as a learning experience, so make sure you don't make hard assumptions on anything until you've tried it at least five times. Or, of course, if you have a dating coach on hand, take his or her advice.

2. **External factor:** Even if you were the best looking, most wealthy and attractive person in the world, this person would've rejected you due to something else you cannot control. This factor could something like the other person is already in a relationship, just got fired from his or her job, or is grieving a recent death. These are extreme reasons why this person rejected you and you must always assume this is the case if you cannot take away a clear "learning experience" from the rejection. Once you are comfortable and confident in yourself, rejection will no longer cause you to evaluate what's wrong with you. You will take rejection if it comes and then promptly move on.

Example Scenario 1:

Recently, I was walking in downtown Boston and my male friend decided to approach a girl on the street to say, "Hello, I think you're beautiful. Can I take you on a date?" She was startled when he tapped her on the back. She looked at him and said, "Uhh, I'm OK, thank you," and ran off. He came back to me with his head down and didn't even want to talk about it.

You might say, "OUCH! That hurts!"

You know what I say? "Awesome!"

Based on my experience, I believe that there may be a few reasons why this girl rejected my friend:

- He approached her from behind and startled her (learning experience).
- He was too forward with his romantic intent by asking her out on a date right away (learning experience).
- She was late for work and couldn't talk (external factor).
- She's in a relationship and felt uncomfortable telling him so (external factor).

The reality is that we will never know the real reason. In this case though, my friend should try to grow from his learning experiences and try a different approach next time.

Having approached thousands of women in my life and experienced almost every scenario you can imagine, I now thoroughly enjoy rejection. Rejection is my friend. If I'm going out and every interaction I have is going extremely well, I'm clearly not pushing myself enough to meet higher-quality people.

Example Scenario 2:

I've noticed that women are much more sensitive to rejection than men are. Another friend of mine recently met a guy at a party and felt they had a really close connection. She gave him her number and literally spent the next week waiting to hear from him. The text or call never came. She just didn't understand why he wouldn't call her, and attributed it to him not thinking she was pretty enough. In this particular case, there was absolutely no way to know "if she did anything wrong" and she just had to assume that it was due to an external factor.

Your own beliefs about yourself control
your perception of rejection.

We all have a tendency to believe that if we get rejected, it's because the person doesn't like us or because we're ugly. They don't like how we look, how we talk, our chubby cheeks, our big ears – whatever insecurity you have, this is the reason you think you were rejected. The most transformational shift you will make as you continue to build your self-esteem is telling yourself that when someone rejects you, they are missing out on their one opportunity to meet you, and so they are making a grave mistake.

Once you get to a point where rejections are as fun as successes, you will be able to take an enormous amount of pressure off of yourself. Whenever a painful event occurs in life, our brains instinctively search for the most logical cause of that pain so we can avoid it in the future. Most of our brains in this situation would tell us that to avoid feeling bad about ourselves, we must stop overextending our boundaries. In Scenario 1, my friend will probably think twice before approaching another woman because he's automatically associating "personal rejection" with talking to new people. In Scenario 2, the girl will probably be far less open to meeting men and giving them her phone number. These are not productive corrective actions to take after being rejected.

The trick is to continuously remind your brain that the rejection you've experienced is just a learning experience or the result of an external factor. Before you know it, you will be laughing at rejection because it's a fun opportunity to learn more about yourself and others.

The unfortunate reality of dating is:

Initially, the negative effects of rejection might outweigh the positive effects of acceptance.

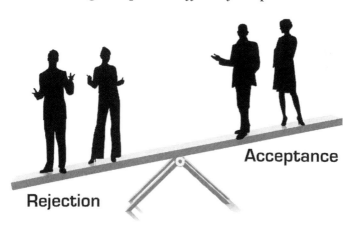

Acceptance

Rejection

If you go around and approach ten people in a night and nine of them love you while one of them rejects you, I'm sure most people would go home and feel great about their night. Unfortunately, this is not a common ratio to encounter, and even if you're doing *everything* right, only about 20% to 30% of the people you approach will be interested in you – even if you're at a venue specifically for singles. The numbers are even more stacked against you if you're approaching people for conversations at cafés, grocery stores, or at social gatherings. Rejection comes in many different forms, and the only thing that really matters is your perception of that rejection.

At first you will get rejected many, many times. Even when you're getting some positive results, the negative results will still hurt. As you improve and continue to practice, you'll notice that the seesaw will get more balanced and before you know it, the benefits of acceptance will far outweigh the negatives of rejection. Once this happens, your self-esteem become less and less vulnerable to the whims of other people.

Just know that we all get rejected and it's nothing personal. Now let's put all of this into perspective.

Putting rejection into perspective

Your life is nothing but a mere speck on the timeline of Earth's four billion years, and let's not even get into the age of the universe. Billions of people have died before you, and the only thing that is truly certain in life is that you will die eventually, too. Also, for 99.999% of us, no one will ever care to know that we ever existed after we've been dead for a century. It's just the reality of human existence.

> *Don't over-exaggerate the importance*
> *of certain events in your life.*

Think about it – a ten-minute conversation is nothing but $1/3,679,200^{th}$ of our life. Odds are, regardless of how mind-blowingly memorable it is, you will probably forget about it within the month or year.

If it goes well, so what? If it goes poorly, so what? Most of the time, it will amount to nothing, so stop thinking that everything matters so much.

It's usually not possible to be able to predict which events in our life will actually have an impact on the rest of it. How many times have you made a seemingly small decision and it turned out to be the choice that changed the course of your life forever? Or, alternatively, how many times did you think that a certain event in your life would have a huge impact, and it ended up having a very small result instead?

Just stop thinking about the potential importance of your social interactions. Unless you can gain a learning experience from your interaction then just put it in its place as one of the most insignificant events to take place on planet Earth.

It's not the end of the world! It's not the end of your dating life! It's just a healthy part of living.

I love thinking about life through this lens. It takes all the pressure off of me to succeed and creates an enormous pressure for me to *do*. Why does it matter if I succeed when it really doesn't matter in the scheme of this world? When you want to go and talk to someone new, just remember this piece of wisdom from my good friend Russell:

I'd rather regret doing it than regret not doing it.

You can agree or disagree with this statement. That's really not the point. The point is that it's imperative to start focusing on the success of just doing something rather than the potential consequences of it going badly.

Do you ever have those moments when you *know* you want to go talk to someone but you just wuss out? Then you get home and think, "Why didn't I just say something?" If you take on the philosophy of preferring regretting *doing* it to regretting *not* doing it, then you'll experience far less regret in your life. It's rare that you'll regret approaching someone, especially as you increase your self-esteem, because you begin to grow a thicker skin to rejection and the positive experiences you have in life become far more important to you than the negative ones.

Think about this the next time you question yourself about talking to a certain someone at a party or social gathering.

Now let's take a look at how naturally attractive people think.

"Natural" belief systems

A *natural* is a man or woman who is great at attracting others without having studied or learned how to do it. Most people think that naturals are just "good looking" people. However, there are many people who are naturally very good at building attraction that do not possess strong physical attributes. Alternatively there are good looking people who are not great at attracting others. So, regardless of your physical attributes, you can absolutely transform your ability to attract other people.

Society tells us that you've either got "the goods" or you don't. If you're a natural, then you get everything in life, and the rest just have to just realize that they don't have options as to who they end up with. This is absolutely not the case and I've worked with dozens of people who at a first glance you wouldn't think would be great at dating or attraction. After putting some time and effort into their dating lives, these same people now have the option to be with any type of person they've ever desired. It all stems from their own self-esteem and belief systems.

It's all about your own interpretation of yourself. Take this scenario: Imagine you're walking down the street and a group of five men or women look at you and started giggling. If you're a natural, you would assume that they are giddy about seeing you and think you are wildly attractive. Now jump back into your shoes. What are your assumptions? Many people who are unsuccessful in dating would just assume they're being laughed at because there is something wrong with them. (The first thing someone might do is to run to the bathroom and make sure they don't have any boogers in their nose!)

This is the difference between a natural's personal beliefs and a non-natural's personal beliefs. Our beliefs about ourselves and our interpretations of events are reflections of our self-esteem. So the real question is, why do naturals perceive the same exact scenario so much differently than non-naturals?

Our past experiences dictate our interpretations of events.

Typically naturals started out in life on the right foot. For one reason or another, they were very well accepted when they were younger which gave them confidence later on in life. They may have been cute, talented, or good looking when they were younger, making them the center of attention, and causing them to be showered with praise and rarely scolded. This builds strong self-esteem and confidence, which results in success with attraction later on in life. Starting out life on the right foot will undoubtedly give you strong self-esteem in dating and attracting others. Naturals have had a history of success in attracting others so they interpret events positively as well.

Now I want you to imagine yourself as someone who is a *natural*. Imagine your upbringing and how it might have been different if you were treated like one. What would it feel like to have lived day-in and day-out during your childhood and teen years having this super power of attraction over other people? Now, imagine taking the brain of that natural, and putting it into your body. Would this person have greater success in dating and attraction? Yes. Would they have a higher degree of social freedom? Absolutely!

How you see yourself is how the world sees you.

My job is to change how you perceive yourself so that you represent yourself as a natural. Our minute-by-minute decisions are driven by everything we have learned in our lives since we were just young children. Those who were fortunate enough to be naturals were reinforced with the belief that they can attract other highly attractive people. So if you begin seeing yourself as attractive, others will also begin to see you this way as well. You can't fake this, though; it must become a core belief. Remember, it's how you see yourself that's important, not how others see you.

Every human being is a unique person with a fresh perspective to offer the world. Because you are a human, you are innately attractive to others. It's just a matter of realizing that you possess unique traits and need to begin exposing them to the world.

In order to ingrain this as a personal belief, you must realize that:

Past experiences ≠ future results.

Everything negative that's happened in your past means nothing. The past does not equal the future and you have the ability to change yourself for the better at any given time.

So I'm not asking you to prove yourself to anyone. I just want you to *realize* that you are an unbelievably attractive person because you are a unique identity. Regardless of where you rank in the 1-10 scale physically, you can create the same level of attraction with those around you by believing in yourself and reversing all of the unproductive beliefs you've been taught since you were a young child.

Negative self-talk

We all have it – it's that darn voice in the back of your head that is constantly dictating what you do and when you do it. It's that part of your brain that tells you that you'll look stupid, that you sound dumb, that you could never get that guy or girl. Ultimately, it's our protector from the feeling of embarrassment. This voice exists as your defense mechanism from harm, and you need to realize that:

A.) It's not going away

B.) It's usually irrational

If you can overcome this voice you will open yourself up to far more success with meeting new people and being confident when you meet them.

I was once having a really rough day and was finding it difficult to get into a social mood. Then one of my friends called me out for being a "Mr. Pickles" because I was being anti-social. I actually got a really good laugh from it. It changed my mood and I was somehow able to talk to people more easily after having a giggle. From then on, I called my inner voice Mr. Pickles. I have conversations with him any time he tells me not to do something that I know I should do. He represents my social anxiety.

Once you begin to have conversations with this negative voice you will notice that it immediately begins to subside.

Create a name for your inner negative self-talker and have a conversation with it. Your rational mind will almost always win when you actually have a real debate with your Mr. Pickles. So long as you can transform the argument from an emotional discussion to a logical debate, you will win.

As you continue to expose yourself to socially uncomfortable situations, try to get this voice to explain why you shouldn't do something. Is it rational?

The Social Freedom
FIGHT

Mr. Pickles   Adam

For example, before I get on stage to give a speech to a large audience, I'll have a dialogue like this with my voice:

Mr. Pickles: Don't go on stage! You're so nervous that your voice will quiver and people will be able to tell.

Adam: My voice will only quiver if I focus on my voice quivering. I will sound strong and confident because I am prepared.

Mr. Pickles: When you first walk on stage, you will trip and fall and it will be awkward for everyone!

Adam: Honestly, when is the last time I just tripped and fell when I was walking? Why would that suddenly happen at this given time? If it does happen, I will get up and deliver the most inspirational speech anyone has ever heard.

Back and forth Adam will battle Mr. Pickles. In the end though, Adam will almost always prevail because he is **rational** and Mr. Pickles is **emotional**. Just keep in mind that logic will always trump emotion when it comes to expanding your social freedom.

Here are some tips on how to create a great persona for your negative voice:

- **State breaker:** It is so ridiculous that it makes you laugh even when you're in a stressed mental state. My Mr. Pickles wears a funny hat.
- **Very visual:** You should be able to picture it very easily and have a clear idea of what it looks like.
- **Negative implication:** Pickles are ugly, green and bitter. Just like my negative voice.

As I mentioned earlier, remember to just have fun and never let Mr. Pickles win the argument.

This concept goes along with the "picture everyone in the room in their underwear" theory. Whenever you feel as though you sound dumb or look stupid, just push it aside and remember that the person you are talking to is probably having the same thoughts. Are you harshly judging them based on their every thought and action? No!

So chances are they are not doing the same to you. Don't punish yourself for certain actions or things you say. Regretting one thing will hurt your ability to move forward confidently. Don't linger on embarrassment: Take it with a grain of salt and move on.

Exercise:

Brainstorm 3 ideas for a negative voice. Follow the steps above to create your own:

Brainstorm 1:_____

Brainstorm 2:_____

Brainstorm 3:_____

Choose the voice that best resonates with you as being your negative voice.

Draw a picture or find an image of him or her on the internet.

Draw or paste a picture of your negative voice here:

Mental state management

The level of your mental energy permeates every means of communication. High-energy people don't literally have "lots of energy"; they are the type of people who *work hard* to captivate, motivate, and engage their audience. We are all capable of controlling our state at any given time; it just takes practice and extreme focus. By focusing on increasing your energy you will be improving your own beliefs about yourself because other people will be more receptive towards you.

My first goal when I set out two years ago to learn attraction was to approach 1,000 women in one year. If you break down the numbers, it means that I consistently approached twenty strangers a week, and especially after a few months, the interactions would last anywhere from twenty minutes to an entire evening. I had to go out almost every night to achieve this goal and the one thing that was constantly slowing me down was my mental state before going out. I would be tired and "not in a social mood," but I knew that I had to meet my goal so I pushed on. By regulating my mental state, I far exceeded my goal.

After three months of approaching women, I had the most unbelievable revelation: Regardless of my mental state at the beginning of the day, after approaching a few people I would become high-energy and ready to conquer the day (or night). It became like clockwork until I got to the point where I was *never* low-energy before social scenarios.

Here are a few critical tips to be able to consistently heighten your mental state:

Get yourself out the door!

The most effective way to control your own mental state is to set an outcome goal for what you're trying to achieve in dating. Break it down into nightly behavioral goals and get yourself out the door. Taking this first step is truly the most difficult and the biggest barrier to improvement. At first you should only really focus on the *behavior* and not so much the outcome. Let me break this down:

- **Behavioral goals:** Consistently taking short-term action to achieve an outcome. For example, if you wanted to lose weight, it would be to run four miles a day five days a week. This is a consistent behavior aimed at achieving the outcome of losing weight. In dating, the short-term action would be to talk to ten new people a week.

- **Outcome goal:** This is the long-term end result. In the above example, it would be losing twenty pounds. In your dating and social life, it would be to find an incredible boyfriend or girlfriend and to build strong, healthy relationships with people.

Basically, focus on what you need to consistently do *now* to achieve your ultimate goal. I would recommend reviewing your behavior goals every day and reviewing your outcome goals every month or so. If you review your outcome goals too often, you can get discouraged. For example, if your behavioral goal is to approach three new strangers a week, and your outcome goal is to get two dates a month, during some months you might have *no* dates and while during others you might have four. Just keep up with the behavior and eventually you will be able to get to your desired outcome. If the behavior is consistently not helping you achieve your outcome goal, then perhaps it's time to try a new strategy.

Warm up your brain!

Our brains are not always "on" because we try to conserve our energy during the lulls and save it for times when we need it. The problem with approaching strangers is that at first it's not fun and usually you are not in the mood to do it. The best way to get past this is by "stretching your brain" before going for the "run." Once you are out the door, here are seven ways to immediately boost your mental state for conversation:

1. **Move your body:** Shake your body uncontrollably! Move your arms and legs, shake your head, and twist your waist – shake every part of your body for thirty seconds.

2. **Act goofy:** Make five different animal noises for one minute as loudly as possible. At first try this in the comfort of your own home, and then give it a try outside in front of a few strangers.

3. **Throw-aways:** Go outside and as you walk by people just smile and say hello to everyone you pass. These are considered throw-aways because you're not going to actually start a conversation with anyone; you're just throwing around "hellos" to get yourself talking.

4. **Activate your voice:** Most of us have seen that part of *Anchorman* when Will Ferrell says "Unique New York" before he begins reading the news. I know it might

seem ridiculous to take social cues from Ron Burgundy, but switch between high and low inflections saying "Unique New York" for five minutes and your voice will be ready for action.

5. **Give compliments:** Give people genuine compliments as you walk by them. For example, "I love your T-shirt," or "Your purse is very cool." Just keep walking as you get your brain warmed up. Receiving smiles from strangers never fails to get your brain energized.

6. **Give five people high-fives:** Everyone that's worth talking to laughs when you ask for a high-five. This will build your confidence as you make people laugh.

7. **Asking directions:** No one will reject you if you're just asking them for directions to the local Starbucks. This gets you used to approaching strangers without running the risk of rejection.

These exercises help you boost your own self-esteem because you're engaging your brain in activities that it's not used to, and proving to yourself that you can try new things with success.

Exercise 1:

Set two outcome goals that you would like to achieve in your dating life.

Outcome Goal 1:_____

Outcome Goal 2:_____

Set two behavioral goals for each outcome goal (total of four behavioral goals):

Behavior Goal 1: _____

Behavior Goal 2: _____

Behavior Goal 3: _____

Behavior Goal 4: _____

Exercise 2:

Rate your brain energy level right now (1 – extremely low energy, 5 – average, 10 – extremely high energy).

Rating:_____

Stand up right now, go out and complete one of the above activities. Rate your new brain energy level:

Rating:_____

Building Confidence

Through Body Language

We've reviewed your self-esteem roadblocks to successful dating, and now it's time to build your **confidence**. The best way to build confidence is through knowledge and practice. Just by reading this book and mastering the techniques presented in these next few chapters, your confidence should increase substantially. Just keep in mind that you're developing the tools you need to help you build attraction with those around you – and most people never even begin the journey of self-discovery you're already on.

A critical piece of your newfound confidence will come from learning how to express yourself well in social situations. This section doesn't tell you *what* to say; instead, it teaches you *how* to say the things you want to express.

Have you ever heard the saying that 93% of communication is nonverbal? Credible psychologists and other experts continue to prove that nonverbal communication is key, yet most people pay very little attention to their body language. One of the most important things you can take away from this book is how to improve your body language and develop your nonverbal communication skills.

Learning how to walk (well)

The way we carry ourselves reflects our unique personalities and styles, and projects our different levels of confidence to the world. It's no surprise that a primary way to express your confidence is to show it in your style of walking. It's important to make sure your walk is deliberate and that it presents a positive image of you to others. Here are a few critical tips to improving your walk:

- Walk tall with great posture.
- Keep your head high.
- Keep it loose and don't be stiff.
- Slow down! We have a tendency to walk faster when we're nervous. Strut like a model.

The best thing about changing your walk is that it's something you do all day long, so you can practice improving your walk anywhere, anytime. Try different ways of walking when you're by yourself or while you're walking to the supermarket. (You don't have to practice this in front of your friends or at work until you're completely comfortable with it). Pretend that you're a model or a famous actor walking down the red carpet. How would you walk if you had paparazzi flashing cameras as you strutted past? Keep this in mind to help you develop a confident style as you practice throughout the day.

Body positioning while standing

When you initially meet someone in any social situation, it's critical to establish a close connection as soon as possible. Have you ever met someone and just felt like you've known him or her forever? A lot of this has to do with the sense of comfort that person is projecting on you through body language. When you meet someone for the first time, try the following things:

- **Keep an angular stance:** Stand basically shoulder-to-shoulder with a slight angle towards each other. Speak to the person as if you're speaking side-by-side with your best friend while overlooking the ocean.

- **Keep an appropriate distance:** Keep about six inches to a foot of space between your arms while you're in normal conversational stages. When you're making a strong statement, lean in slightly; when you're reacting to a strong statement, take a slight step back. Be animated, but try not to invade their personal space. If you get too close to someone without building strong attraction first, you'll come off as creepy and uncomfortable. Body language is all about building comfort!

- **Don't lean in too much:** When we're attracted to someone, we have a tendency to lean in when we speak to him or her as a way to seek affection. If the other person is not yet attracted to you, this will come off as clingy behavior and will hurt your chances of building a sense of comfort and attraction.

- **Take up space:** If you're in a crowded room, don't let yourself get squished. Use your arms to literally push (slightly) against the crowd around you to create space. Make it clear that your environment doesn't control you – it's the other way around.

All of these body language techniques help to portray you as a person with confidence, self-esteem and social freedom. Next time you're at a social gathering try to find someone who looks like they're a natural and see if they follow these guidelines. Observe and emulate their body language to improve your own.

Building comfort and setting time constraints

Although it may not be possible in all social venues, you should try to find a way to sit down with a person to build "comfort" between the two of you. This communicates that you're willing to invest in each other for a longer period of time, and it gives you privacy so there's less of a chance of being interrupted by your friends.

However, try not to directly *ask* the other person to sit down with you. Instead find a reason to sit down. For example, you could say, "I want to show you this picture on my phone – come here for a minute," and just sit down. The other person will naturally sit down next to you.

Flirting without comfort is just a short-lived conversation.

If you think that the person won't be comfortable sitting with you then you could preface the move with, "I really need to get back with my friends, but before I go, I want to show you something on my phone." This technique is known as a "time constraint," which communicates that it will be a short conversation, and put the other person at ease. One of the worst things you can do is make someone feel like they're going to be in a potentially confrontational or socially awkward situation they can't get out of.

Always try to give the other person an "out" in case they no longer want to speak with you before sitting down with them. This is not so that they can actually leave you, but instead so that they *feel* like they can leave at anytime without pressure. Other examples might be:

- "I'm going to be leaving soon but…"
- "I have to wake up super early tomorrow morning so I only have a minute…"
- "My friend should be arriving any minute, but…"

Then, when you end up hanging out for a long time, typically the other person will say: "I thought you had to leave?" Assuming the interaction is going well, you can just tell them that you're enjoying hanging out, so you'll make an exception!

When you're sitting with the person, try to be sitting side-by-side rather than face-to-face. This gives a better opportunity to keep good body posture, touch the person, and to hear the person in loud venues.

Hands

A major problem people have when they meet people is they don't know what to do with their hands. My philosophy about using your arms and hands to communicate is:

It's better to be overly animated than inanimate.

It's absolutely far better to be flailing your hands and causing a huge commotion than to go unnoticed. It's ideal to be somewhere in the middle.

The following techniques should be used:

1. **Clapping:** Making noise with your hands when you reach an exciting moment in your story will add a whole new level of drama to what you're saying.

2. **Keep your hands visible:** Try your best to show your palms to your audience. This communicates that you are open and sincere – that you literally have nothing to hide.

3. **Wave your hands:** This technique can be used to describe visual scenarios.

4. **Use sharp gestures:** Really emphasize certain points using sharp movements.

The standard "still" position for your hands is to keep them at your side. It might feel really uncomfortable at first to put your hands in motion, but just keep trying and it will soon become second nature.

Now here are a few tips on what *not* to do with your hands:

1. **Don't fidget your hands:** This projects discomfort and nervousness. Keep your hands relaxed.

2. **Keep hands out of your pockets:** This is usually telling someone that you're hiding something.

3. **Don't hold your drink over your chest:** It's common at parties or bars for people to have drinks and hold them over their chests. Instead, hold your drink down by the side of your waist. This communicates being "open" to the other person rather than having the drink as a barrier.

Voice tonality

The difference between what we think we sound like and what we actually sound like is astounding. Have you ever recorded yourself on video and watched it? After watching yourself speak, you probably think to yourself, "It seems so strange. I thought I sounded a lot smoother than that!" It's usually pretty embarrassing for most of us to hear what we really sound like

Voice projection is one of the easiest ways to show confidence in what you're saying. When you're building attraction with someone, it's better to say the dumbest statement loudly and confidently than mumble the most intelligent statement under your breath. The former will be far more effective at building attraction than the latter because ultimately people only remember a small portion of the conversation anyways. What they will remember, though, is your high confidence level.

Improving your voice tonality takes energy and focus. If you begin to get lazy with your interactions, the first thing that suffers is your voice inflection. The easiest way to be boring is to be monotone.

The right voice tonality combines the following five attributes:

1. **Speak "uncomfortably" slowly:** We all have a tendency to speak fast, especially when we're nervous and attracted to someone. Focus on slowing down your tempo to the point that you're actually uncomfortable with how slow it sounds. Typically, this is the right tempo.

2. **Sing a song:** Telling a good story is like singing a melody. Your volume should go up and down depending on the context of the story. Show drama and sing the song. Try whispering during certain parts of the story, and raise your voice during others for added emphasis or theatrics (for example, when you're mimicking your crazy Uncle Joe).

3. **Speak clearly and enunciate:** This might seem obvious, but a big mistake that both men and women make

is slurring or not speaking clearly. People fail to enunciate when they're insecure about what they're saying, and when they're just not paying enough attention to the way they speak. And of course, too much alcohol can contribute to this pitfall, too. Remember what I said about booze affecting your ability to attract others?

4. **Vary your volume:** Don't be afraid to speak loudly. It's better to speak too loudly than too softly. Alternatively, once you get comfortable with speaking loudly, try inflecting your voice to go from loud to soft or vice versa when you want to express a clear dramatic shift in a story.

5. **Alternate your talking speed:** By continuously changing the rhythm of your voice you'll automatically create more depth and layers to your stories.

Exercise

If you really want to hear what you sound like when you're interacting with others, buy a digital voice recorder and record your evening's activities. Listen to it the next day and you'll be amazed at how different you sound from what you expect. You'll immediately find new ways to improve your voice tonality just by listening to yourself in natural surroundings.

Eye contact

Establishing clear and resolute eye contact with someone communicates that you're confident and comfortable. More importantly, it indicates that you're trustworthy and have very little to hide. If you look deeply into the eyes of the person to whom you're attracted, then they're significantly more likely to feel the attraction.

The biggest problem is that looking people in the eye is not natural for many shy people. It's uncomfortable and often causes you to lose your train of thought if you're naturally reserved. The reality is that holding steady and consistent eye contact is the surest way to display that you're confident in who you are and what you're saying.

Here's the easiest solution: Don't look them in the eye!

Wait – what? I thought you said –

Yes, I know what I said - but I repeat: Don't look the person directly in the eyes! Stare at the other person's *nose or the bridge of their nose*. No one can tell the difference, and it alleviates all of the discomfort and anxiety you feel when staring someone directly in the eyes. At first you'll think they notice you're staring at their nose, but after trying this a few times you'll be confident that no one is ever the wiser.

Exercise 1

The next time you're walking down the street, make a goal to hold eye contact with at least ten people. You don't need to say or do anything except keep eye contact with them until they look away. Try it on your next jog; it'll make time fly by.

Exercise 2

Have a conversation with someone at work or a close friend and stare at the top of his or her nose for the entire interaction. Ask them at the end of the conversation whether or not they noticed that you were staring at their nose. (I think you know the answer already.)

Smile

It sounds simple, and it is: Just remember to *smile* at all times. This is absolutely critical. Get in the habit of smiling everywhere you go; people will notice it. Looking cool is *not* sitting in a corner trying to look like the models from the movie *Zoolander*. The "blue steel" look is not cool! Looking cool is looking like you're having fun, laughing and smiling all night. People will be naturally drawn to you if you show them pearly whites! If you don't have pearly whites, you're still better off smiling to exude confidence.

The initial touch

The act of touching someone is the most surefire way to flirt. Just remember:

If you're uncomfortable touching someone, then they'll be uncomfortable being touched by you.

So what does this mean? Get comfortable touching people by doing it a lot!

The earlier you establish a physical connection with someone, the easier it is to build attraction and a sense of comfort. Even a simple touch on the arm sends powerful attraction emotions to the other person's brain.

In general, you want to make sure that you touch someone within the first thirty seconds of your interaction. Most people introduce themselves and shake hands to make an initial connection. However, let's not fall into the standard boring trap of tradition! The *high five* is one of the absolute best ways to touch someone for the first time because it:

- Is unique and differentiates you from everyone else.
- Can be changed and enhanced to create your own fun high five/handshake (for example, doing a high five, then pounding fists and exploding. Believe it or not, this is a great way to build an instant connection).
- Shows that you are playful and have high social freedom.
- Can be used with all types of people in all social situations.
- Transfers value to the person you are high fiving (which most people appreciate).

Before I became passionate about dating and attraction, I was a pretty nondescript guy. I sold methods for implementing process improvement initiative software to Fortune 500 companies (I assure you that it was as boring as it sounds). During this lackluster time, I was once attending a conference and met a guy named Dave., Dave was walking around the conference room, giving everyone high fives! I was thinking to myself, "What a goofball!" But I was intrigued by his unique approach to the work environment, so I paid close attention to him that day. I soon noticed that the strangest thing happened when he began to talk to executives: They would go for the high five and laugh hysterically as soon as they saw him. He had them hooked without even saying a word. What Dave's story teaches you is a lesson for life: Get them laughing and you'll win them over!

Facial gestures

There are about ninety muscles in the face, thirty of which exist solely to express emotion. Depending on how you use them, you can express significantly different messages. For example, you can express the following distinct emotions without ever uttering a word:

- Confusion
- Fear
- Humor
- Goofiness
- Excitement
- Mysteriousness
- Interest
- Anger
- Boredom

The list goes on and on, but most of us don't use enough of our facial expressions to add drama to our conversations. This can be attributed to many factors, whether it's a low degree of social freedom or just a lack of energy. In reality, using these capabilities is a rejection-free way to build more interest in what you're saying.

Use facial gestures to depict drama in your conversations.

Exercise:

Get in front of a mirror and take pictures of yourself projecting the emotions listed above. How do they differ? Do you have stories that you typically tell with those types of emotions? Try using these facial expressions to enhance the next story you tell.

Body language: Indicators of interest

It's important that you're observing the person you're speaking with to determine their degree of interest in you. There are certain indicators of whether a person is interested in you, and the most important ones to watch out for are:

- **They touch you:** If someone touches you, this is one of the clearest signs they're interested.
- **They're body is positioned towards you.**
- **They're fidgeting or adjusting themselves:** This typically means they're nervous talking to you or are trying to look their best for you.
- **Making clear eye contact with you.**

Word of caution: If you're speaking with someone and they're not displaying these indicators of interest, it does *not* necessarily mean they aren't interested in you. They could be "playing hard to get" or maybe they're just not very expressive. If you're unsure whether someone is interested in you, my golden rule is that if they're sticking around, you can assume they're interested.

Escalating the touch

So once you've initiated contact with a handshake or a high five, it's time to show interest in the other person with a slightly more intimate touch. There are different levels of intimate touching that can be broken down into the following six categories:

- Level 1: Hands
- Level 2: Forearms
- Level 3: Upper arms and shoulders
- Level 4: Waist and back
- Level 5: Face and neck
- Level 6: Legs and inner thighs

Notice how this is a hierarchy of which parts of the body humans consider most intimate. For example, rubbing the inner thigh has enormous implications of sex, while stroking a person's face implies a desire to kiss.

If you want to kiss someone, the easiest way to do it is to slowly work up this ladder of intimacy. If someone is comfortable with a neck rub, then a kiss is generally a good next step. Just be sure to watch out for indicators of interest (or disinterest!) as you continue to get more intimate with someone. If you perceive any discomfort, then step back and re-evaluate.

A pet peeve for some people (especially women) is when someone is "touchy-feely" too early on. Women often need to feel as though they're in control of developing physical intimacy, and by occasionally backing off the man gives the woman opportunities to process what's happening and decide whether she's comfortable with continued physical contact.

Conversely, if you're uncomfortable with touching someone at all, be aware that the dreaded "touching chasm" will occur if you let too much time pass without *any* intimacy. If you meet a person whom you really like and have taken on two dates, but you haven't yet made physical contact except for a friendly hug, it will become incrementally more difficult to get intimate as time goes on. The easiest way for a girl or guy to end up relegated to the notorious "friend zone" is by failing to establish a physical connection at the beginning of the relationship.

Modeling positive body language

Another effective way to build comfort with someone is to emulate his or her body language.

Be like them, and they will like you.

For example, if the person is leaning against a wall, then you might want to lean against the same wall; if they're leaning to one side and sticking their other leg out, you might want to do the same.

But remember: You only want to emulate *positive* body language. For example, if you're talking to someone whose arms are crossed, this communicates being "closed off." If someone is doing this when they talk to you, it's your job to do whatever possible to get them to uncross their arms. One way to do this would is to tell a story that requires you to grab both of the other person's hands. (This will allow you to both establish physical contact with them *and* change their negative body language.) Or, you might say something random or silly like, "Hey, I like to play hot hands. Have you ever played? Let me show you how." Another way to change someone's negative body language and create intimacy is to compliment a ring, watch, or bracelet and touch his or her hands as you do it.

Exercise:

Practice touching everyone's hands and shoulders. It's easiest to do this at first with close friends and family to train your brain to do this automatically.

Building Confidence by
Knowing What to Say

People will only usually remember the *best* 20% of what you say and the *worst* 10%. The key to building confidence and attraction is to work on maximizing your best 20%, minimizing your worst 10%, and filling in the remainder with attractive sub-communication (body language). This portion of the book is focused on using words to communicate attraction. Again, it won't focus on the specifics of what to say, but instead it will center on general conversational concepts.

Holding your frame

Picture an intricate painting that from far away shows a cascade of beauty. As you get closer you can see all its fine details, and no matter how you look at it, you can appreciate the painter's creativity. Like this painting, you have beautiful, intriguing qualities that draw people to you. But even the most incredible painting is contained within its frame, and has a finite limit. Like a fine painting, you, too, have limits that encapsulate who you are.

Staying within this frame is staying true to yourself. Straying from your true identity can sometimes seem like an easy, "cheap" way to build attraction with someone; we've all fallen into the trap of saying insincere things we think another person wants to hear.. For example, imagine that a woman is interested in man and somehow they get into a conversation about sports. She says she hates sports.

The guy responds by saying, "Actually, I'm a huge baseball fan and will never miss a single game."

Since she likes this guy, her natural tendency is to respond by saying, "Yeah, well, I could get into baseball. Maybe I just haven't given it enough of a chance!"

However, by responding this way, she's contradicting her previous statement and also demonstrating that she's willing to immediately sacrifice her own enjoyment to try to make him happy. Although this might be true, it's generally not a good idea to communicate this when you're first meeting someone.

When you're trying to build attraction, it's critical to hold true to a strong **frame**. Your frame is what dictates your boundaries, and once you establish them, it's critical to stand by them as you would a strong opinion. In the above case, the best response the girl can have is:

"We would *never* get along. We should totally just walk away from each other right now!" (Using a *very* sarcastic and playful tone/body language stance.)

By responding in this manner she sticks to her guns while still building a connection with the guy. This would build attraction with the man even if he usually only likes girls who like sports. That's because her reaction shows confidence in who she is, and makes it clear she's not willing to arbitrarily sacrifice her interests and opinions for the sake of another person's enjoyment.

From this point, the girl should change the conversation topic to something they might both be interested in. By continuously changing the conversational flow to agree with your frame, you're sending signals to the other person that you are strong, confident, and have a well-defined Unique Concise Identity. Once you've built the emotion of attraction you can revisit the sports conversation and explain that you'd be open to trying new things.

Of course there are many circumstances that should cause you to be flexible, and you should really use your discretion here. But I assure you that it's better to have too *strong* a frame than too *weak* a frame. We all have the tendency to have a very weak frame when we talk to people to whom we're attracted, so make it a point to have a much stronger frame than is comfortable.

Building routines and stories

Have you ever told a joke more than once to a different group of people? Of course! If it works well once, why not tell it again? If you don't yet realize the full impact of a good story or an off-the-cuff joke, then you're missing out on huge opportunities for social success.

Do stand-up comedians make up their material on the spot? Absolutely not! They have practiced the same material hundreds of times and have tried many different variations of each story to make sure their delivery is perfect. The same thing applies to public speakers and actors. It takes a lot of *hard work* to be charming, funny, outgoing, confident and dramatic.

Treat all of your conversations like performances. Everything we say and do is a performance, except that usually we need to

93

improvise and come up with new material on the spot based on the reaction of our given audience. The reality is that you can portray yourself as even more naturally funny and charming just by putting thought and effort into your stories before going out and telling them.

Telling a story to build attraction is slightly different from telling a generally funny or interesting story. To tell a story to build attraction, follow these guidelines:

1. **Use emotional words:** How do you feel? How do the characters in your story feel? What are they smelling, hearing, tasting, and seeing during any given moment in the story? Most importantly, how do they react to these sensations?

2. **Convey your understanding of social value:** We'll get into more detail on social value later in this chapter, but everyone sits somewhere on the social hierarchy. This is all perception, and as people make assumptions about whether or not you're valuable (make them look cool). To build a sense of your social value say something like, "I was hanging out with my buddy Joe, and he's a successful music producer in Boston." With a statement like this, you're giving yourself value because you know someone who is of a high value and he was willing to hang out with you. The key here is not to bluntly tell people how cool you are, but instead to give subtle hints of your social value.

3. **Include fewer facts:** Too many facts make a conversation boring. Details of the story are more important to you, the teller, than to the listener. Unless they add value to the story, leave facts out.

4. **Use characters' names:** This might seem contradictory to the previous statement, but names add personality to

your story's characters and allow the listener to imagine your story more clearly. Make your listeners feel like they're *living* the story.

5. **Incorporate elements of surprise:** There's an element of surprise in any good story, and it's crucial to build suspense before the surprise is revealed.

Here's an example of a girl telling a story without keeping these tips in mind:

"So I was driving down East Hampton Street yesterday on my way to work with my friend, and we knew there was something wrong with my Honda. It seemed like the car was shaking or something and I pulled over and my tire was flat. It was so annoying, we had to wait like two hours for the tow truck to come and change the tire for us."

Now let's see how her story sounds after applying the principles learned above:

"So I was driving down the street yesterday with my friend Jamie, and she was telling me about how she's opening a new club downtown. I was completely ecstatic to hear that she's really making it in the world, and then, out of nowhere, I began to feel this thump (hitting your hands together). I was terrified, and I smelled tar and gasoline but I had no idea what was going on. It gave me such an intense rush of adrenaline. I could see that the car wasn't handling too well, so I pulled over. There was nothing wrong with the body of the car; I checked under the car, nothing under there. And then, I walk over to the back right and there it was (pause) – a *flat tire*. We had to wait around for a few hours for the tow truck to come but it gave us a ton of time to talk about how I might get involved in the opening of Jamie's new club."

95

Do you see the difference between these two stories? Here's what's different the second time around:

- She removed the useless facts of the street name and the type of car.
- You can *picture* her friend Jamie in the car next to her.
- You're impressed (consciously or subconsciously) that she is friendly with someone who is opening a club. Notice that the story doesn't say that *the girl herself* is opening a club, only that she associates with high value people like Jamie.
- It's easier to feel the situation for yourself as she uses words like "terrified" and "adrenaline."
- She built up suspense before finally revealing what was wrong with her car, making the story more exciting and intriguing.

Notice that just by applying some of these storyline techniques even an excruciatingly boring story can become intriguing and dramatic.

Exercise 1:

Write down one short story below that uses all of the components of a compelling story. It can be about anything, as long as you use the principles outlined above:

_____
_____
_____
_____
_____
_____
_____

Exercise 2:

Keep track of stories you tell that get positive reactions from people. If you think that there might be merit to a story, take a quick note of it (immediately, so that you don't forget it!). Go home that night and write out that story word-for-word as it flows from your head. Once it's written down, apply the principles in this chapter to improve its effectiveness. Compile at least three compelling stories and begin telling them when you're interacting with people.

When to tell certain stories

I love it when people tell me that they "never have anything to say to people when they first meet them." The reality is that we all lead fascinating lives. Your life may not seem fascinating to you because you live it day in and day out, but the content of your everyday life can actually serve as excellent fodder for a compelling story. As long as you tell your stories using the techniques above, you'll be able to captivate your audience no matter what.

The reality is that you can tell the story you came up with in Exercise 1 at any given time in a conversation. One of the most interesting things I noticed when I was consistently approaching strangers was that they really didn't care how "random" my stories were. They actually didn't even notice whether or not my stories tied into the conversational thread; people just love a good story! Just use one of the following lead-ins to begin telling any story you have in mind:

- "That's funny because…"
- "A similar situation happened to me when…"

- "I know what you mean, because just the other day I was..."

Find a way to weave your routine stories into the conversation. If your story is compelling enough, people won't care why you're telling it, and they certainly won't think twice about whether it follows the vein of your previous conversation. Have you ever been in the middle of a good conversation when someone suddenly says, "Wait, what were we talking about? How did we get on this subject?" That usually happens because you've become so engrossed in an interesting topic that neither one of you can remember where you started – and that's a good thing!

Are they flirting with you?

Hundreds of dating experts around the world have tried to define exactly what flirting is. It's such a strange form of sub-communication that it can be hard to explain! Sometimes you know without a shadow of a doubt that you're flirting, but aren't really sure what it all means. The most interesting scenario is when people are unsure whether a person is flirting with them. Earlier in the book we reviewed indicators of someone's interest in you, but the best mentality you can have to increase your confidence is to realize that:

If someone you're interested in is talking to you, then that person is flirting with you.

"Naturals" have this mentality; why shouldn't you? You must always assume without a shadow of a doubt that the person you're speaking to is interested in you. Now it's time for you to learn how to flirt effectively. As you read the next section, keep this important tip in mind: Never wait for someone to make it a flirtatious conversation – instead, lead your interaction in the direction you want it to go!

How to flirt

I flirt all day long. I flirt with my audience when I speak, I flirt with all the women I meet, and yes, I flirt with men if I want to make them like me. This book talks a lot about how to build attraction – which is essentially how to flirt with someone effectively –, but this section is focused on how to **flirt with words**. There are obviously many levels of flirting, but any effective flirtation is accomplished using the following four techniques:

1. **Charm**: This is a quality possessed by those who listen well and lead conversation in positive directions. Being a good listener doesn't mean letting someone drone on endlessly about their horrible workday and other boring aspects of life. Rather, a good listener will open up conversational threads that are funny and exciting, and then sit back and listen to the other person's reaction. To be charming is to know how to drive the direction of a conversation where you want it to go without doing all of the talking.

2. **Sarcasm:** Being sarcastic in a positive way requires a certain degree of restraint: It's not great to be categorized as an outrageously sarcastic person, but using sarcasm in the right amount can be extremely effective. Sarcasm is flirtatious because it shows the person that

you're comfortable enough with them to tease them while showing that you're witty and quick.

3. **Mysteriousness**: Being mysterious and evasive about "standard" questions is the easiest way to flirt with someone early on in an interaction. We have a tendency to always want to give away every part of ourselves to prove that we're worthy of someone wanting to know us. The hard cold truth, though, is that people generally don't care about you within the first few minutes of meeting you. They're basically testing you in those first few minutes to see if you're worth their time. To pass this test, you need to come off as mysterious and interesting. For example, if a girl asks me what I do for a living, I might say, "I'm actually a hand model," and start dancing my fingers on her hands (remember the importance of touch!). I'll say this as a joke and then move on in the conversation. She can find out later what it is I actually do for a living, but I know that creating a bit of mystery makes her view me as an interesting challenge.

4. **Humor: Just** like being attractive, being funny can be a learned skill. Many of my friends will attest to the fact that I'm not a guy who tells jokes, but I've learned how to make people laugh and certainly know how to be perceived as the jokester when I first meet people. This is certainly not a book on how to be funny (although I recommend reading one or two and taking a comedy class), but I want to offer some tips on how to develop your sense of humor. The easiest way to be funny is by making social observations and acting outside of the social norm. Here are a few examples:

a. **Observation:** Point out people in the room and analyze them based on what they're wearing: "She totally just came from band practice."

b. **Being silly:** Point out a piece of clothing that's clearly not something you would wear (like something that's extremely feminine or masculine) and say "Holy crap! I was going to wear that same thing tonight!"

c. **Being outrageous:** Do a "Michael Jackson kick" out of nowhere, and just say, "Yeah, I have a habit of doing that from time to time."

d. **Role-playing:** Playing pretend is always funny **builds a sense of comfort with someone**. For example, if someone says something that you perceive as snappy, you could respond with: "We are so totally broken up. I want my Rob Schneider DVDs back. You can keep the dog, though..." (This obviously needs to be delivered playfully and with sarcasm!)

e. **Group cold reading:** A cold read is when you make a playful snap judgment about a person or group of people. For example, going up to a group of people and pointing to each person and saying, "You're clearly the trouble maker, you're the nice one, and you're the playful one of the group." Then if they ask why, just point out an article of clothing or an observation about each that could potentially lead to that judgment. Even if your judgments are way off, they're still funny! Sometimes, the less accurate your read, the more people love it.

101

f. **Leveraging inside jokes:** Creating inside jokes will undoubtedly be funny and can be used later for "call-back attraction" in texting or calling.

These are all silly and nonsensical ways to be funny, but each technique sends a message that you're comfortable with yourself. If you're naturally funny, go for it and test the boundaries. Just make sure you don't become the entertainer of the night – your end goal is to build attraction and not just be the class clown. Also, these types of ways to bring humor to a situation typically show that you're not trying too hard, and that you're just playful. Only telling jokes the whole night can come off as trying too hard, and no one finds that attractive.

Whenever you're talking to someone you're interested in, make sure you are conveying charm, sarcasm, mystery, and humor. At first you might overdo it, but don't worry! It's always better to do too much than too little. Get comfortable with flirting first, and then if you find you're *consistently* coming off as too intense, you might want to tone it back a bit.

Social value

Highly desirable people are attracted to leaders who are of high social value. Are you attracted to empowered people? Most people are.

If someone spends more than a few minutes with you, then they want something from you. If they feel that by talking to you they will gain value from you, then they will surely want to continue talking to you and see you again.

Having high social value is simply the
adult way of being "cool."

If you want to build immediate attraction in a social scene very quickly, the easiest way to do this is to quickly establish your social value as an **alpha leader**. If you can establish yourself as having enormous social value very quickly, you will immediately become highly desired by others.

Imagine a nerdy looking guy with a plaid sweater sitting completely by himself in the back corner of a bar. There is a live band playing, and the entire bar is going wild. After the second song, the lead singer jumps off stage, approaches the kid in the corner, and gives him a hug like they are the closest friends in the world. How would your image of him change? You would immediately think to yourself, "Hmmm, how do they know each other? He must be pretty awesome if he knows the lead singer of this band. I want to talk to him!" What's actually happening is that the lead singer is transferring value from himself to the dorky kid in the back of the bar. And who knows? The seemingly dorky guy could be the director of the band's recent award-winning video. You never can tell.

This is an extreme example, but there are microcosms of this happening in every social gathering. Interestingly enough, even though it's so prevalent, we fail to notice that all of this "coolness" is merely a perception and can be *enhanced* for our own benefit.

If you don't know anyone at a social venue and people don't know you, then you're typically starting out with average-to-low *perceived* social value (like the dorky film director in the back of the bar). Generally most people won't notice you and people won't feel that they can gain value by talking to you. However, if you're that same person and have a five-minute conversation with the manager of the venue when you walk inside, your value is immediately increased. From there, it's even easier to talk to a group of strangers because you've been validated by your relationship with the manager (people really do notice these things in social scenes!). It's a steppingstone, and so long as you build up your value consistently through-out the night, you will become one of the coolest people at the venue.

What should you say to people at the beginning of the night to build your value? Anything! You could be speaking to the manager about how much you love (or even hate) his estab-lishment. You could speak to the bouncer about the big line at the bar next door. Just create an image of high social value. If you're at a party, then talk to the host of the party first. In any social venue, the organizers are typically the highest value people. So go out there and meet them.

> ***Build social value by getting socially***
> ***validated by other people.***

For example, I recently entered a party and followed my three-second rule (I need to talk to a stranger within thirty seconds of walking into any new setting). I approached a group of four people; two men and two women. They immediately shunned me as an "outsider" and were very cold to me. In the corner of my eye, I noticed a group of two girls I knew from high school and we greeted each other with open arms. I want you to visualize our body language, our tone of voice, our pres-ence at the party.

After my brief five-minute interaction with the girls from high school, I walked past the original group of four people and they said, "Adam, where are you going? We're ordering a pitcher, you want in?" This was a classic example of those girls from high school handing over value to me as someone who was "cool" just because I knew them. In reality, the only reason I knew them was because we went to high school together, but this proved enough to the other group of people that they accepted me into their group.

Unfortunately, we don't always know people at every social venue. But as long as you're *displaying* that you're social and know people, then you'll raise your social value. Your social freedom skills (covered in the following section) will kick into overdrive during the first few interactions, and you'll notice that as you continue through the night your interactions will become warmer. The following techniques will help you build your social value in one night:

- **Go to a social scene with perceptively high-value people:** These can be naturals or just other cool people. If they know other people there, then all the better.
- **Meet lots of people in a night:** I would rather have 10 two-minute conversations in my first hour at a social scene than have 2 ten-minute conversations. By the end of your ten conversations, you can go back and reengage with the most interesting of the ten people you've spoken to. You've also built an enormous amount of value in the room by portraying that you know a lot of people. This not only increases your options of who to go back and speak to but also makes your conversations much warmer when you decide to finally get to know people better.

- **Merge groups of people together:** If you're in the middle of a conversation with one group of people, and another group of girls or guys walks by, you can leverage your value from your current group to talk to the new group of people. For example, if you're speaking to two people and another two people that you're interested in walk by, you can immediately draw them into your current conversation. You will almost always be received more warmly in this situation than if you were by yourself.

The last point to keep in mind is:

> *Being of high social value is important, but not being of low social value is mandatory.*

If you are *removing* value from a group of people or a person you've approached, you're guaranteeing rejection. No one wants to look un-cool, so make sure that you've built up your own value to at least neutral status before approaching people you're attracted to at a social gathering. An example of being perceived as low value would be going to a bar with ten other hugely obnoxious people screaming and causing a commotion. If you hung out with this group for an hour and then tried to go out and meet new people, it would be infinitely harder than if you were alone. Once you're associated as having low value in any social scene, it's an uphill battle.

Having a high degree of social freedom will surely allow you to build your social value more easily. Just remember that if you approach ten new groups of people in a night, and five of them reject you, your social value will still be net positive. People will generally notice that you're being social and even if they notice you getting rejected, they will judge you based on how you react to that rejection (your self-esteem) rather than the fact that you're getting rejected.

But much of what I've told you won't make any difference at all unless you increase your social freedom beforehand. This next section teaches you how to build social freedom to add to the tools you've already learned to help you build your self-esteem and confidence – and ultimately attain improvement and success in every aspect of your life.

Exercise 1

Go to a social venue and observe everyone very closely. After about ten minutes, point out (in your mind) the three highest value people in the room. Ask yourself, "Why are they high value? What are they doing? Do they have a high degree of social freedom?"

Exercise 2 (for the dedicated)

Approach one of the high-value people in the room and begin a conversation. Immediately after the conversation, find someone else nearby and begin a conversation with that person. Notice how your second conversation was immediately warmer because you've been awarded value already.

Building Your Degree of Social Freedom

What is Social Freedom?

Having a high degree of social freedom is being able to speak, feel and act like your true self in any social situation without fear of criticism, rejection or failure. It's a matter of being outgoing and social with people without concern for breaking social norms.

Social freedom is simply being comfortable in unfamiliar or uncomfortable social situations. You'll never be truly confident in yourself until you learn how to manage yourself in awkward moments and how to control the environment around you. When you're socializing and expanding your comfort zone, you will undoubtedly be exposed to uncomfortable situations, and it's important to control how you react to that discomfort. For example, if you approach someone and then realize that their boyfriend or girlfriend is right next to them, then you're in a potentially awkward situation. Your degree of social freedom will dictate how you react to these types of situations.

The only way to become comfortable in all social situations is to bring out the true you by consistently exposing yourself to uncomfortable activities. This will give you a thicker skin to break through social barriers.

The strangest thing about unveiling the true you is that you might not even know the type of person you are until you've really exposed yourself to enough people and social situations. It's difficult to know what you're truly capable of until you expand your own comfort zone.

Social freedom is critical to being successful in dating because it will help you to meet more people, be more confident when you meet them, and not fear rejection every time you say, feel or do something outside of the social norm.

Social freedom is essentially the polar opposite of *social anxiety*. Imagine if you lost the part of your brain that censored all your thoughts and inhibitions. What would you be like? How would you act around others? What would your true personality be like? Chances are that it would be different than how you act today with most people.

Note: Having a high degree of social freedom doesn't equate doing everything your brain tells you at every moment. There is a natural filter in your brain for a reason, and it should never go away completely. The only problem is that social anxiety can be a major inhibitor to doing things that will make you most successful in life such as approaching the person of your dreams or confronting your boss for a pay raise. The true benefit of increasing your degree of social freedom is that you will always have a *choice*. Being able to choose when you want to say, do and feel things will inevitably allow you reach your own goals in life.

Here are a few examples of having a high degree of social freedom:

- When a sales person is taking advantage of you, you tell him, "Hey, I see what you're doing and you better stop right now before I call your manager over here." Confrontation can be difficult without social freedom.

- When you smell strange perfume on your boyfriend's jacket, you have the freedom to confront him. If he's cheating on you, you have the freedom to walk away from the relationship.
- When you're at a party and you're wildly attracted to someone, being able to say, "Next Monday I'm going to the park, and you will be the perfect person to come with me."
- When you're at a supermarket and notice someone wearing a T-shirt with your favorite band on it, you approach the person saying, "I *cannot* believe you are into MGMT! You and I are totally meant to be!"

Get the drift? Being able to open your true self up to others is the one sure-fire way to become:

- **Outcome-independent:** Not concerned with that actually happens in your interaction, but instead just satisfied that you did it.
- **Flirtatious:** When and where you want to be.
- **Unique and compelling:** It takes social freedom to be different than other people.
- **Outgoing:** Being fun and playful when you want to be.
- **Comfortable with rejection:** Less concerned about what other people think about you.

Essentially, social freedom is the common thread sewn through every concept in learning attraction. The sharper your needle, the easier it will be to knit your sweater of attraction. I want you to genuinely be *you* because this is the only way that you will find the right partner. By increasing your social freedom you will:

- Meet more new people and thus have more romantic options available.
- Be more confident to expose your true self earlier on in social interactions and not waste time.
- Be more attractive because you're comfortable with being unique and different.
- Be more genuine with others during your social interactions.

Lastly, and most importantly, throughout this book you have learned a number of techniques and concepts that can't be applied without a certain degree of social freedom. As your social freedom expands, so does your capability of having effective, attraction-building interactions with others.

Exposing yourself to the elements

Social freedom is something that you can expand infinitely over time. The reason I named my speaking, coaching and product company **Ultimate Social Freedom** (www.UltimateSocialFreedom.com) is because I see "ultimate" as the level that we should all be constantly striving to achieve.

The only way to track your improvement is to make note of where you are now, so you can see how far you go. Some people are just naturally outgoing. We all know them; they're the "life of a party" because they're completely comfortable with themselves in social settings.

We all have our own social phobias, and they will never go away completely. But you can manage them by continuously exposing yourself to the elements of society and striving to reach Ultimate Social Freedom. If you're exposed gradually to uncomfortable social situations such as performing in front of large audiences, then you'll learn how to cope with rejection, failure, and criticism.

In order to gradually expose yourself to socially uncomfortable situations, you need to understand the two types of social freedom:

- **Absolute social freedom** is your "average" level of social freedom over a given period of time. In general, how do you cope with socially uncomfortable situations?

- **Relative social freedom** is your degree of social freedom at any given moment. In a given moment or on a given day, how will you be able to deal with a socially uncomfortable situation? Social freedom fluctuates from day to day and moment to moment.

Take following scenario as an example: You get someone's number at a party and you're very interested in them. Your absolute social freedom dictates how you *generally* feel about calling new people on the phone for the first time. Your relative social freedom dictates how you feel *on that given night*, in that particular instance. Your absolute social freedom can be expanded over time if you begin to get used to calling people regularly, and your relative social freedom can be expanded if you mentally prepare yourself for the call. Both are equally important to making yourself more outgoing, confident, and increasing your ability to deal with seemingly uncomfortable social scenarios.

Expanding absolute social freedom

Expanding your absolute social freedom is just like going on a diet. When you first decide to go on a diet, you think that you should stop eating everything and starve yourself. Well, we all know that this isn't a sustainable strategy and generally after a week we're running to the local Baskin-Robbins for our double-fudge ice cream cone with extra M&Ms. Binge dieting doesn't work, and neither does binging on exposure to uncomfortable social situations.

If you expose yourself too quickly to your social and dating phobias, you'll react intensely and go back to your old habits rather than facing your fears. For example, if you're the type of person who is nervous about talking to a stranger on the street for five minutes but you force yourself to speak in front of three hundred people in an attempt to face down your social anxiety, you're trying to break through your social boundaries too quickly! The problem is that you haven't been prepared enough by frequent exposure to such situations, and you'll probably end up feeling so uncomfortable that you'll never try it again.

When you learn how to snowboard, you don't go on the double black diamond trails first, you start on the bunny slope. The key to a healthy expansion of social freedom is to gradually increase the area of your comfort zone so that you're prepared for rejection or failure if you don't succeed.

The way to begin consistently increasing your absolute social freedom is to ease yourself out of your comfort zone and develop a thicker skin against the pain of rejection. These two steps will bring you closer to unveiling the true you because you'll be more comfortable showing the world your true personality once you've lost your fear of rejection and discomfort.

For the sake of this lesson, I will categorize people's social levels into three categories:

- **Socially Anxious:** This is the state of suffering emotional discomfort, apprehension or worry about *normal* social situations, interactions with others, and whether you're being evaluated or scrutinized by other people.
- **Socially Normal:** This is the state of being comfortable in *normal* social situations. Most people fall in this bucket.
- **Socially Free:** This is the state of being able to say, feel, and act like your true self and to be *unique* in social situations (normal or abnormal) without fear of rejection or scrutiny.

Notice that I've used the terms "normal" and "abnormal" in the above explanation. It's important to remember that different social groups and cultures have their own rules for what's considered normal in society. Because each social group is different, being socially free is about being able to observe the norms of the group you're in, adapt appropriately, and then push the social boundaries of that particular group so that you're considered unique.

In order to succeed in this area of your self-improvement, it's imperative that you begin to define your own social freedom plan for growth. Although this isn't a science, I'll try to make this concept as tangible as possible. The list below outlines certain activities along with the social freedom levels necessary to complete those actions:

- **Socially Anxious:** Make eye contact with a stranger walking past you.
- **Socially Anxious:** Ask a cashier where to find milk at a grocery store.
- **Socially Normal:** Ask someone for directions.

115

- **Socially Normal:** Make small talk with a Starbucks barista for thirty seconds.
- **Socially Normal:** Do a little dance in the streets when you hear great news.
- **Socially Free:** Sing karaoke in front of strangers.
- **Socially Free:** Give a speech at a friend's party or wedding in front of 200 people.
- **Socially Free:** Approach a man or woman you're attracted to.
- **Socially Free:** Give a presentation to over 1,000 people on a subject you're unfamiliar with.

(At www.SociallyFreeTV.com you can take a survey designed to formulate your own accurate Social Freedom score.)

The best way to continuously expand your absolute social freedom is to stretch your comfort zone slowly but surely by working your way up through a hierarchy of challenges. Setting a very clear plan for yourself and your social goals will ensure that you'll be able to improve your absolute social freedom threshold over time. If you do these exercises twice a week for three months, your absolute social freedom threshold will increase and you'll become significantly more socially free.

Exercise:

Complete as many of the following social freedom exercises as you can. Take note of your comfort level during the exercises (0=Couldn't do it; 1=Very Uncomfortable; 5=Normal Comfort; 10=Loved doing it!)

Exercise	Actual 1-10
1. Make eye contact with five people you don't know as you walk by them.	
2. Ask a stranger "What time is it?"	
3. Ask a stranger the weather forecast for the day, and then small talk for a minute.	
4. Make small talk with a waitress/waiter even if they are busy.	
5. Skip around in public and flail your arms.	
6. Approach someone (man or woman) on the streets and spark a conversation. Hold the conversation for at least two minutes.	
7. Give three high fives to random strangers.	
8. Dance around a group of strangers that you don't know.	
9. Approach a man/woman you're attracted to and say ANYTHING (ask for directions, the time, where she's from…etc).	
10. Give a presentation to a group of ten or more people on a topic that you are familiar with.	
TOTAL	

Add up your total score and this is your social freedom score. Visit www.SociallyFreeTV.com to see where you fit on the spectrum of socially anxious to socially free.

Note: Your expected score is almost always higher than your actual score! Doing these types of activities is never as hard as you think they'll be. If these particular activities are too easy or too hard for you, create your own social freedom expansion exercises. Set a goal to do them a certain number of times a week.

Expanding Relative Social Freedom

Relative social freedom is your social freedom threshold at any given moment. If I told you to approach the man or woman of your dreams right now as you're reading this book, would you be able to do it comfortably? Probably not, because you're not in a social mood (I'm assuming this because you're reading a book and not out socializing). The key to expanding your relative social freedom threshold is to learn how to get yourself into a social mood at any given moment.

There are a few sure-fire ways to increase your relative social freedom threshold:

- **Call an old friend:** Get yourself into a talkative mood by calling an old friend and catching up. Surrounding yourself with good friends who are positive can really increase your confidence and social freedom. These people are more likely to give you an honest outside perspective of your social traits, and therefore give you valuable information about how others view you.

- **Envision your interactions:** Give yourself a strong mental picture of exactly what is going to happen during your interactions on a given day. Only picture positive results and omit any negative thoughts (tell Mr. Pickles to be quiet). Visualization can be a very strong technique for increasing your social freedom threshold at any time.
- **Give 3 high fives to strangers:** This is guaranteed to get a laugh and will get you in a fun mood.
- **Try a new technique from the body language section:** If you try this in a socially anxious or socially normal situation, it will get your brain functioning in a more social way. For example, if you're not great at holding eye contact with people, then find someone to have a quick conversation with and make it a point to hold eye contact the entire time. This will get your mind into a social state.
- **Focus on your breathing:** Taking deep breaths for one minute can calm your nerves and get you focused on the task at hand.
- **Complete some activities from the previous section:** This will get you moving and get your brain into a social state. For example, just go up and ask a random person for directions to the local subway. After any interaction your social readiness will automatically increase.

If you want to expand your absolute and relative social freedom skills, it's really just a matter of getting out the door and making it happen. Remember what I said at the beginning of this book:

Just get out there and make things happen…today.

Approaching people

As you can imagine, having a high degree of social freedom makes you much more comfortable with approaching people. Both men and women can approach anyone they want at any time. You are the only person who's stopping you from meeting more people. Learning how to approach complete *strangers* will undoubtedly help you to gain more confidence when you approach people in other social situations (such as at a friend's party). When you begin to approach strangers, the first thing you'll notice is that people are much more receptive to meeting you than you might think. This is especially true when you're confident and comfortable with yourself while doing it.

Trust me, I understand firsthand that it's against every cell, every muscle, and every thought in your body to go up to a complete stranger and start a conversation. I used to have a serious fear of approaching women, but through consistent exposure and practice I no longer have this fear at all.

Before I learned more about dating and attraction, every time I was interested in someone romantically, I used to think it made sense to go up and say something along the lines of, "Hi, I'm interested in dating you. Do you want to go out?"

For some reason our brains automatically assume that we should always tell people our intentions right off the bat.

This is why 99% of us don't actually say *anything!* Because we assume that we need to put ourselves "out there" within the first few minutes of a conversation, we're daunted by the idea of interacting with people.

If you're having problems approaching someone you're interested in, then (at first) approach them in a way that's considered **socially normal.** This could be something such as asking directions, asking them where they got a certain article of clothing, or where they got the drink they're holding. The social freedom exercises listed previously are a great place to start to get comfortable doing things like this.

Soon you'll realize that approaching strangers really isn't that strange at all. People want to meet new people! As you become more comfortable with approaching strangers, you'll eventually approach someone you're attracted to – and you should do this in a unique way.

Here are a few easy conversation-starters that can be used anywhere, anytime:

- "I'm looking for an authentic Italian restaurant in the area. What's your favorite place?"
- "Excuse me, do you know where I can get a delicious hot chocolate/iced coffee?"
- "Hi, I totally know you from somewhere. Summer camp? High school? You look very familiar…"

As you can see, these are pretty socially normal questions or statements (some with a bit more flair than others) because what you say is far less important than how you say it. If you say any of these things to a stranger and are comfortable and confident in what you're saying, then usually people will be receptive to you.

What's most important here is that you're saying *something*. Just get comfortable with saying something – anything – and you have conquered 90% of the battle of approaching new people. Don't create artificial roadblocks for yourself; it's really not that complicated once you try it a few times!

Once you get past the initial fear of just saying something, it'll be time to really start spicing it up a bit to make your approach more unique. Here are five different types of conversation-starters for you to think about:

- **Opinion:** Ask someone for an opinion on something a little outrageous. For example: "Excuse me, I need a guy's opinion on something. Are Uggs sexy?" Then, you might always want to have a continuation on the subject such as, "I actually happen to think men's Uggs are sexy. You look like the type of guy who wears men's Uggs. Do you own a pair?"

- **Situational:** Make a comment on a particular relevant situation. For example, if a large group of girls are screaming at a social gathering, you could say, "What do you think: birthday party, bachelorette party, or fake bachelorette party?" You could follow up with, "I think bachelorette party because one of the girls walked by and she smelled like man stripper."

- **Cold read:** Make a snap judgment about the person. For example, if they are at a bar and order a Jack and Coke, you could say, "I get this feeling about you that you're a total badass." You could follow up with, "Everyone I've met that drinks Jack and Coke seems to be a rebel."

- **High-impact, backhanded compliment:** Say something that raises your value in the conversation and could almost be perceived as an insult to the other person. These are hit or miss! If someone "gets" the joke, then they'll be very interested. If not, then prepare yourself for rejection. Here's an example: "You look very familiar to me – were you on a 2:00 AM infomercial last night?" Then you could follow up with: "You look like the guy/girl who was selling those juicers on Channel 9, you were very compelling, I almost bought it but it looked like a cheap product." Usually they'll respond with a laugh saying, "I don't know if that's a compliment or not."

- **Direct:** Be upfront about your intentions. I don't always recommend this for beginners because you need very strong body language skills to build attraction with this conversation starter. As long as you don't look desperate, you can pull this one off. An example would be, "Excuse me, I was just walking by you and I would've completely kicked myself in the face if I didn't say hi, and yes, I can kick my own face. Anyways, hi."

As I mentioned, there are a million things to say and I've tried and tested dozens of conversation-starters myself. I still only use a select few that work best for me. It's better to master two conversation starters than to know a dozen of them and never use them. What's most important is that you are exuding confidence, high self-esteem, and a high degree of social freedom.

The key components to a good conversation-starter are:

1. **It's unique:** The person has never heard what you're saying before.
2. **It breaks the ice:** You're actually saying something! Don't waste your time learning conversation -starters

that you know you will never say. Don't limit yourself to simple ones, either.

3. **It has a punch line:** There's a punch line and the person doesn't know what you're going to say before you say it.

4. **It's fun or funny:** If you're not a naturally funny person, make sure what you're saying is fun, light, and playful.

Exercise 1:

Write down three conversation-starters that you would feel comfortable saying (either from above or your own):

1. _____
2. _____
3. _____

Exercise 2:

Set a behavioral goal as to how many times you will approach someone using each different conversation-starter.

Behavioral Goal: _____

Remember to try every conversation-starter at least five times before you stop using it. What you're saying might not be the problem, so keep at it!

Evolution of approach anxiety

Why is it that approaching a complete stranger is absolutely terrifying for the vast majority of us? Our fear of getting rejected from others is one of the strongest fears humans have. It's called **approach anxiety** and both men and women suffer from it.

I can assure you that when I first began this journey, even the *thought* of approaching someone on the street made my stomach turn. Every worst-case scenario in the world would run through my head and my body would feel an enormous physical response, including a rush of adrenaline, muscle tension, blushing, and even nausea. I would imagine that if I went up to a girl I liked and said something, then at least one of the following would happen:

- Her boyfriend would be there, and as a *result* he would kick my butt.
- Everyone would laugh at me, and as a *result* no one would talk to me for the rest of the night.
- I'd freeze up, and as a *result* the girl would push me away.
- I'd say something wrong, and as a *result* the girl would slap me.

While I've faltered in all these ways, the *results* of those failures have never turned out to be as bad as I thought they would. For example, I've actually made a few guy friends after having approached their girlfriends! I've had a group of people laugh in my face and in twenty minutes they're all my best friends for the night. Our brains always exaggerate the consequences of rejection and the only way to build social freedom is to get some experience under your belt.

So why do we feel this intense anxiety even though the results are never as bad as we think they'll be? The reality is that this extreme anxiety you feel before meeting new people for the first time is something that has been a part of our DNA for thousands of years.

Think about this scenario.

Targus the caveman is fifteen years old in 10,000 BC and lives in a tribe of about fifty people. Everyone of course knows each other very well and this one tribe is their whole world.

On one fine morning Targus wakes up and decides that he's going to find his mate. He makes a goal for himself and says, "No matter what, I'm going to do whatever it takes to find a female!" He does the math, and knows that there are six eligible females in the tribe.

He approaches the first one and says, "Me, you, mate now!" She is disgusted and runs away from him.

He brushes it off and moves onto the next, "Me love you!" She turns her back to him.

He moves onto the third and says, "I am…" and is interrupted by her saying, "No!" She had already heard the news from the other two women that Targus was aggressive and no one was interested in him. She wanted nothing to do with him because why would she want someone who has already been rejected by two other women?

Moral of the story? None of us are descendents of Targus! He never had his chance to procreate and became an outcast from his tribe. At the ripe old age of thirty, he died, childless.

So what happened? Targus used a high degree of social freedom in approaching every woman in his tribe, but unfortunately in those days, we were not rewarded by this trait because there were such a small number of people in tribes. If you were perceived as having "low social value" in your tribe, then no one would want to procreate with you. So what happened? Our brains developed a defense mechanism that basically told us to stay within the boundaries of being socially normal to ensure replication of our genes. So keep this one thing in mind:

We are no longer bound to tribes.

Our brains are ancient and have not adapted to urban society, so we have to remind ourselves that there are over 300 million people in the United States and very few of them will find out if we're rejected or embarrassed by a certain social situation. No matter what happens to you, there are always other tribes. Unlike the way it's been for the past hundred-thousand years for humans, we now have the ability to continuously reinvent ourselves as we meet new people.

If you're stuck in a "tribe" (such as high school, very small college, or your office environment) and this has been your only means of meeting people romantically, it's time to make a change. The key to building your social freedom is to feel as comfortable as possible being the completely uninhibited you, and unfortunately this is very difficult when you're surrounded by people you know well. The best way to do this is to find places to meet people where you can be totally *outcome independent* (the outcome shouldn't matter to you, just the fact that you did it). Examples of places to meet new people are:

- Shopping malls
- Parks
- Bars
- Grocery stores
- Music/sporting events
- You name a place, you can meet people there!

Once you build your social freedom, confidence, and self-esteem, return to your tribe and you'll be amazed at how differently and more confidently you interact with them. They will be too.

Learning how to change

For the true you to surface, you must **learn how to change.** It's true. For change to happen in your life, you must change yourself first. You wouldn't be reading this book if you weren't looking to improve your social life, and the only way to increase your degree of social freedom is to improve your appearance, your communication style, and your identity until the shoe fits. Building your social freedom is an adventure of self-discovery:

By discovering others, you will discover yourself.

So many people drop out of dating self-improvement programs because they say, "It's just not *me*." I hate to break it to you, but you don't *know* "you" until you've given it a chance to surface. The "real you" is actually just the product of a lifetime of rules, social norms and family influences. Keep in mind that you only have an average of about seventy years to live on a planet with about seven billion people. You'll never *really* get to know the entirety of your capabilities because there are literally hundreds of different paths your life could take. So with all that said, you will need to experiment quite a bit to find one path that allows you to expand your confidence, self-esteem and social freedom.

Case study: Emanuele

Let me tell you a story about someone I admire greatly; he's a true social freedom phenomenon. His name is Emanuele and he's originally from Italy. I had the opportunity to meet Emanuele very early on in my learning about dating and attraction and he has been a guiding force for me ever since. When I first met him, we were both determined to improve this area of our lives. His strength ended up being his absolute fearlessness in any social situation. He has come as close as I've seen someone get to reaching Ultimate Social Freedom. He thrives on continuously pushing himself out of his own comfort zone no matter what the consequences might be.

I was once sitting at a restaurant with Emanuele and we were talking about social freedom. Our conversation went like this:

Adam: "Is there anything that makes you feel socially uncomfortable?"

Emanuele looked around the room and said: "Going up and talking to that group of girls would make me nervous." He then pointed to a group of twelve beautiful women sitting at a restaurant celebrating what seemed to be a birthday party.

Adam: "Well, you know what you have to do now…" This was a game we would always play: if you say that it makes you uncomfortable, then you have to go do it! There's no choice.

Emanuele: "OK, fine." He got up out of his chair immediately, walked over to them, grabbed a seat nearby, and said: "Who's the lucky birthday girl? I'm the hired entertainment for the day."

And then I heard it – a burst of laughter that engulfed the entire room. They loved him, he loved it, and he instantaneously made twelve friends simply by:

- Not hesitating for a single moment.
- Projecting confidence.
- Sitting down without asking for permission.
- Saying something completely unique and high impact.

The waitress at the restaurant came up to him and asked if he would leave the table for a minute so that she could take orders from the women. He said OK and walked back over to our table.

Adam: "Good job! How'd that go?"

Emanuele: "You know what, that actually didn't make me feel uncomfortable!"

So what can we learn from Emanuele's story? Social freedom is something you can learn. He was not always socially outgoing and was by nature shy and introverted. However, he worked very hard at improving this part of himself and is still continuously pushing himself to achieve a high degree of social freedom. Learning to enjoy your expansion of social freedom will take you very far in life – even beyond dating.

Emanuele's mantra is:

Embarrassment is an emotion that only you feel.

It's only an emotion and it won't kill you. The more you feel it, the more you get used to it. So get out there and experience everything the world has to offer.

Post Attraction

Now that we've covered how to build attraction in an interaction by increasing your self-esteem, confidence, and social freedom – and by using your Unique Concise Identity as your foundation – let's go over some of the logistics of what to do once you've built attraction.

Getting the digits

Both men and women build up the act of "getting a phone number" into being one of the most awkward and difficult things in the world. Women typically feel uncomfortable telling a guy to take down her number if she likes him, and guys grimace at the thought of asking a girl for her number. Here are a few tips to help you manage the act of exchanging digits:

- **Don't ask – tell!:** If you want to see someone again, then be forward and say so; don't ask them for it. For women, tell the guy to take down your number. This portrays confidence and self-esteem. For men, just say that you want their number.
- **Call them immediately (or have them call you) when you get the number:** Always make sure that both people have the name and number stored in each

other's phones before you leave the interaction. This saves the dreaded response text of "Who is this?" when you reach out to them later.

- **If possible, plan the next meet-up:** It is infinitely easier to get someone's number if there's a purpose for it. For example, if you're both interested in art, you might suggest, "You know what? I think there's an art exhibit next week that we should check out. Let me get your number and I'll give you a ring." If you have no common activities yet, the easiest way to do this is to say, "I might be having a get-together next week, you should totally come."

- **Send a text that night:** I highly recommend sending a "Nice meeting you tonight" text at some point that same night. You don't have to get into a long text conversation, and you can wait a few days afterwards before texting/calling again, but this is a good way for them to remember you. If possible, use "call back" humor from an inside joke that you may have with the person. This will give them something to remember you by.

- **Funny last name:** If the person is programming your name in his or her phone, have him or her put in your last name using alliteration or maybe a joke you talked about earlier. For example, I'll have a girl put my name in her phone as "Awesome Adam" or "Adam Attitude," depending on the conversation. The next time you call/text them it will immediately bring back good memories of your interaction.

Just remember, if the person you're talking to is of "high value" in the dating scene, he or she has been asked for their number numerous times before. This is not new to them and is not awkward for them as long as you're comfortable with it. Just do what makes you feel comfortable and they'll most likely reciprocate with a positive response.

Exercise

Set a goal for yourself for the amount of numbers you want to give out and/or receive in the next month.

Goal:_____

Following the hierarchy of communication

With the internet, cell phones, and the prevalence of social media sites, there are many different levels of connection between people in today's world. In the dating world, the following hierarchy represents interest (level 1 is the lowest, and level 9 is the highest):

1. Texting
2. Facebook friends
3. Emailing
4. Chatting on Facebook
5. Talking on the phone
6. Meeting in person
7. Touching
8. Kissing
9. Sex or Marriage

Now, this is clearly not to say that you can't skip multiple steps, but people generally feel comfortable with following these steps to build a sense of connection. In some situations, it's advantageous to skip a few to show confidence; on the other hand, skipping an important step can look as if you're trying too hard or are completely over the top. This is a judgment call on your end as to how attracted to you the person is.

When you're ready to reach out to the person meet up again, it's very important to build attraction again. A lot of people think that just because you had a great initial interaction and you built attraction, that it still exists when you call or text them a few days afterwards. I would recommend initiating the attraction again by using one of the following techniques:

- **Call-back humor:** Referencing a funny/interesting moment in your initial conversation.
- **Confusion**: Saying something confusing or random to elicit a confused response. Make sure you have your response ready to go. An example might be: "Hey, I'm off to Guatemala for three years, just texting to say goodbye."
- **Being playful**: "Oh my god, I just saw a rabbit out my window and I thought of you."

Be sure to display mystery, excitement, and confusion at first when you're trying to reengage someone for the first time as this will be far different than anything they've ever heard before. Just be different. aI do *not* recommend initiating with the following:

- Hey there, what's up?
- How are you?
- What's happening?

Remember, the emotion of attraction can fade away very quickly after your initial interaction, so be sure to remind them of your confidence, social value and social freedom. Be different!

First "meet-up"

If you haven't noticed, I don't like the word "date" because traditionally it has a number of negative connotations to it, the first of which is the notion that it's a "serious" exchange. (It's kind of ironic that I'm known as a "dating coach," huh?)

Traditionally, on a date the woman is judging the man, and the man is trying to impress the woman. All this does is put up a very real barrier between both of you that would never exist if you knew each other within a different context. How are you supposed to get to know the real guy if you're forcing him to do extravagant things just to get your attention? How are you supposed to attract the woman if you're trying to buy her affection?

Make your date as non-traditional as possible.

The general rule for both men and women who are going on dates is to make them fun, mysterious, and exciting. I have a friend Jessica who was using an online dating site, and would go on two or three dates a week. She kept complaining about how the guys were always so boring! I then asked her where she would go on the dates and her response was, "It's a rule that the first time I go out with a guy it needs to be for dinner at this restaurant right near my apartment. It's the most convenient for me after work." That was the problem! The dates were boring because they were so traditional. I told her to just let the guys decide where to go for the next few dates.

It took a few more boring dates, but she stuck gold with my advice. The third guy she went out with took her on an adventure she would never forget. Before meeting up with her he sent her a text that said:

"Meet me at the corner of Commonwealth and Beacon at 8:00 PM. Wear sneakers, jeans and bring some paprika. Let's go for an adventure tonight."

She had no clue what the heck this guy was talking about but was insanely curious. I mean, why the paprika?

He picked her up and took her to the Boston Museum of Fine Arts for a new exhibit that just opened up. The sneakers and jeans were for comfort and the paprika was just a joke. He was being playful with her and just telling her that this was not a normal "date." It was mysterious, exciting, and funny all at once.

Jessica told me that they were running around the museum like they were on a sixth-grade field trip. Most importantly, they were just being themselves; no structure, no "serious" talk, no impressing one another. They fell for each other. It was the best time she had ever had on a "date" and there was no dinner or alcohol involved.

In summary, break the rules and do something unique. Here are a few suggestions for first time meet ups:

- A day in the life of you (take the girl/guy around your neighborhood).
- Go to a farmer's market.
- Go to a park and bring toys and games (Frisbees, bocce, Scrabble).
- Jump in the car and "see where you end up" (I recommend always having a backup plan just in case you end up nowhere interesting!).

- Go on an errand together (going grocery shopping can be pretty hilarious if you let it).
- Check out local events, art exhibits, festivals, carnivals, outdoor concerts, etc.

Above all, just make it fun and unique. This is why I don't recommend going on traditional dinner dates:

Dinner dates automatically give a "serious" tone to any date. Also, eating with someone you don't know very well can be awkward for both people. Be different.

It's more common for men to take the lead in deciding where and when to go on a first date. For men, if you feel uncomfortable doing this at first, then perhaps give two options for the girl to choose from. Women typically don't want to have to make these decisions; they want to be able to *judge* you based on what you decide to do. If the woman has her heart set on dinner, I would seriously recommend telling her that you already have dinner plans but would like to meet up afterwards. Trust me, after you take her out on the most exhilarating night of her life, she'll be so much happier that you were able to skip all of the formalities of a dinner date.

For women, don't let guys take you on traditional dates! The easiest way to get out of the "boring date" funk is to just tell the guy ahead of time, "This last guy took me out to dinner and it was super awkward the entire night. Let's do something really fun. You decide." This is when you can really judge the guy on his creativity.

If you're stuck on the idea that a date is not a date unless dinner is involved, try and think back to why you think this

137

way. Maybe you've never tried anything different. Maybe it's just what you've always seen on television. Don't be afraid to break this "social norm."

Exercise

Based on the suggestions above, research your town and find three activities to do on a date that are non-traditional.

Activity 1:_____

Activity 2:_____

Activity 3:_____

Thinking About a Relationship?

Deciding on commitment

One of the biggest mistakes that both girls and guys make when they're dating is investing their time in the wrong things. Einstein (and also my father) once said, "The definition of insanity is doing the same thing over and over and expecting a different result." As you follow the attraction techniques and strategies in this book you should get to a point where you have lots of options of people to settle down with. This is a "rich man's problem" – it's a good problem to have! It can be very, very difficult to make the choice of whom to commit to for a real relationship.

Be sure to analyze your logic and see how it matches up with your gut. Your logic will produce a prioritized list of people that you might want to commit to, and your gut will usually only give you one. If your logic and your gut agree, then it's clearly an easy decision.

If they clash, try to find the reason why your gut is telling you to go in a certain direction. Is it only because of the intense sexual attraction you're feeling for the person? If so, have your fun, but maybe it makes sense to just keep it casual. Then ask yourself why it's illogical. The best you can do is weigh the pros and the cons. Sometimes, making a list can help you through this analysis.

Word to the wise: Don't let your attraction for someone dictate your every move and make you commit to someone whom you know is not right for you. Just remember, attraction can be a learned skill, so just because you're attracted to someone doesn't mean that they're right for you.

Meet the right person at the right time

If you're not ready for commitment, then do *not* force it.

*Relationships are all about meeting the
perfect person at the perfect time.*

Leave time to focus on yourself. You'll know when it's the right time to meet the perfect person, and once it's time, I assure you, that person will come along. As you continue to build your self-esteem, confidence and social freedom, you'll realize that it's not necessary to commit to the first person you're interested in. It's OK to play the field and meet lots of people.

I believe strongly that our journey in life truly begins in our twenties. This is when we have an opportunity to "Do me" – as in, be ourselves. No longer do you have to go to school, live at home, or live the life you've been told to live. So many people forget that it's OK to just be yourself for a while, and get to know who you are. Discovering and exploring your spouse will be far more fruitful, exciting and enlightening if you've had a chance to truly explore yourself first. Whatever you do, just don't rush into anything.

How to keep them attracted

Have you ever heard the phrase, "I'm now in a relationship, time to take the uniform off?" *Wrrrrong attitude!* If anything, it's time to change into your sports gear, because you'll be working harder than ever to please your partner once the initial honeymoon period passes (usually after the first six months or so).

The worst thing you can do is get too comfortable and lazy with your girl or boyfriend. When you apply for a job, you try to look your absolute best to present your strengths for the job. If after six months on your job you start wearing a tank top every day to work (unless you're working in construction) your days are numbered. You need to always exceed your target at work to be promoted. The same goes with relationships: Your partner always needs mystery, always needs excitement, and most importantly, always needs to feel *attracted* for the relationship to grow. If the relationship stops growing, it's usually dying.

It's amazing how the little things you do will keep your partner loving and caring for you. The best words you can say to begin a conversation with your partner are, "I was thinking about you earlier today and..." A huge majority of people get so caught up in their everyday lives that they forget to give their significant others the attention they clearly deserve. And then holidays and birthdays come around, and they try to make up for the lack of attention by buying them gifts and showering them with attention. Not only does this *feel* forced, but in reality it *is* forced.

Just remember, the more effort you put into keeping your partner attracted to you, the more love and affection you'll be given in return.

The most important thing to keep in mind for the rest of your life, whether or not you're in a relationship, is:

Be attracted to yourself to live a life full of love.

About the Author

Adam LoDolce graduated magna cum laude from Bentley University and immediately began a lucrative career consulting for Fortune 500 companies. Upon realizing that his newfound wealth and professional success failed to bring him happiness and a healthy social life, he committed himself to the study of dating and social techniques. After countless hours of trial and error, Adam finally found he had discovered the secrets to building confidence and leading a life of social achievement.

Adam now lives in Boston and shares his formula for success by dedicating his time to a career as a motivational speaker, dating coach and author. His work brings him around the world to conduct workshops and deliver keynote speeches to colleges, high schools, associations, and conferences. His topics of expertise include building self-esteem, improving confidence, expanding social freedom, and learning how to date, build attraction, and live a life that's socially free.

His one-on-one live and virtual coaching practice helps men and women of all ages and backgrounds achieve ultimate success in their dating lives and beyond. His unique approach teaches accessible techniques to conquer social anxiety and unleash the true identities of his clients.

If you're ready to take control of your life and change for the better, visit www.UltimateSocialFreedom.com for more information on Adam's speaking engagements, his areas of expertise, and a full list of products and programs designed specifically to improve your dating and social life.

He is also the producer of www.SociallyFreeTV.com, a video website that provides free advice and forums to singles around the globe.

33232740R00087

Made in the USA
Charleston, SC
08 September 2014